Other Books by EUGENE T. MALESKA

Sun and Shadow

Three Voices
(with Arthur Bramhall and Herman Ward)

The Story of Education
(with Carroll Atkinson)

Simon and Schuster Crossword Book of Quotations Series

Simon and Schuster Crossword Puzzle Book Series
(with Margaret Farrar and John Samson)

The Junior Crossword Puzzle Book Series
(with Margaret Farrar)

The Simon and Schuster Book of Cryptic Crossword Puzzle Series

A Pleasure in Words

Across and Down

MALESKA'S FAVORITE WORD GAMES

*Over 100 exciting, entertaining and eclectic games
from the master of the genre*

Eugene T. Maleska

A FIRESIDE BOOK
PUBLISHED BY SIMON & SCHUSTER INC.
New York London Tokyo Sydney Toronto

Fireside

Simon & Schuster Building
Rockefeller Center
1230 Avenue of the Americas
New York, New York   10020

FIRESIDE and colophon are registered trademarks
of Simon & Schuster Inc.

Designed by Helen Barrow
Manufactured in the United States of America

10 9 8 7 6 5 4 3 2 1
ISBN 0-671-50497-5

Contents

I am indebted to Mrs. Pamela Parsons,
who typed most of the manuscript,
and to my editor, Ms. Patricia McKenna,
whose kindness and encouragement spurred me on.

Foreword

During my checkered career I taught evening classes twice a week at Hunter College in New York City. One of the courses was called Methods of Teaching Reading, and my students were would-be or present teachers of the early grades in elementary schools.

One evening the dean called me to his office. "Gene," he said, "your course in reading methods is so popular that I can't find enough seats to accommodate the applicants. What's your secret?"

I laughed. "Maybe it's because I'm such an easy marker. Everybody gets an A."

"Don't kid me," he said. "I've checked last year's sheets. You have the usual bell curve. So let's have the truth. What's going on?"

"Okay." I took a seat. "We play word games half the time."

"Word games? What's that got to do with reading?"

"Dean," I said, "picture yourself as a small child trying to decipher the hieroglyphics we call letters and words. Also, try to remember that as a child you liked fun and games—if you were normal."

He nodded. "Yes, I was a normal kid."

"Well, my theory is that if we connect the learning and reading of words with lots of fun, we have converted a chore into a pleasant game. The adults in my class are just grown-up kids. I teach the word games to them and they enjoy playing. Then some of them go back and try the games on their children. The ones who are preparing to teach record the games in their notebooks and can't wait to try them out after they obtain their licenses."

I then went on to explain to the dean some of the games. A few of them will be described later in this book. But the one that impressed him most will be related only in the following paragraphs:

Nouns like boy, girl, book, *etc., are the easiest words to teach to a tot. You demonstrate "Tommy is a* boy." *You write* boy *on the blackboard or on a chart. "Mary is a* girl." *Again you write the word. "This is a* book." *You show them the primer and once more you write the word.*

But to demonstrate verbs, adjectives and adverbs, you need action. So perhaps you ask the custodian of the school to find a board. You place the board atop a box full of books. Lo and behold, you have a seesaw! Now you can teach such words as ride, up *and* down.

I once showed teachers of first-graders that the average preprimer contains fewer than twenty words, all of which can be demonstrated via action. It's like the game of charades that we adults play. Variations of that divertissement will be discussed later.

My chief reason for writing this book is to share with you the many word games that I once loved as a child and still enjoy, as well as more sophisticated ones that delight me today. It's my contention that such games not only provide us with fun but also sharpen our minds and expand our vocabularies. In some cases, I will be dealing with old games in the public domain and in other instances I will be introducing you to new ones that you can play with others or by yourself. At any rate, it's my hope that this book will provide you with interesting diversions that may simultaneously help you to forget your troubles and increase your pleasure.

Please keep in mind that it is not my intention to present an all-embracing "encyclopedia" of word games. As the title indicates, these are only my *favorites!*

Pax, amor et felicitas,
E.T.M.

Party Games

FICTIONARY

My all-time favorite party game involving words is Fictionary, a description of which was discovered by my daughter Merryl in an underground Boston newspaper about fifteen years ago. We assume it was invented by some college students.

To play Fictionary you need a small group of trustworthy word lovers, an unabridged dictionary, lots of scrap paper and a supply of pencils. One person is chosen to consult the dictionary and find a strange but legitimate word that it's probable nobody in the group knows. During that period, the host passes out pencils and scraps of paper which must all be the same size and color. In that connection, index cards are perfect for the game.

Now the game is afoot. Let us say that the selector picks the word *gabarit*. He or she then calls out the word and spells it. If one or more members of the group are familiar with the word, the selector must go back to the dictionary and pick another unusual word. Incidentally, it is obvious that complete honesty in the group is essential. Assuming that no one has ever heard of *gabarit,* each of the selector's listeners writes down the word and then creates a legible "fictional" dictionary definition, while the selector writes down the actual dictionary definition on his or her index card. An adequate time limit is set, and then the selector collects all the newly created definitions, shuffles them and mixes in his or her own card.

Next, the fun begins! After carefully examining all the cards to make sure that the handwriting or lettering is legible, the selector labels each card, starting with #1. Then the definitions are read to the group and, if requested, the selector reads all of them a second time.

Using the *gabarit* example, here are six definitions. (Remember that the true one is somewhere in the list.)

1. a firm, durable fabric with a twill weave
2. a sword used by the Saracens
3. a bird related to the magpie
4. a small ship formerly used in Scotland
5. a dark woody plant growing in Africa
6. an outline on a drawing of an object

Note: The true definition is given on page 211. Take your own guess now.

The next step is for each member of the group, except the selector, to name by number the definition that seems to be the correct one. The host usually acts as the scorer. There are various scoring methods, but the one I like best is as follows:

a. Anyone who chooses the correct definition gets 3 points.
b. Anyone whose "fictional" definition is chosen gets 2 points for each instance in which the guesser has been fooled.
c. The selector gets 1 point for each instance in which the correct definition was not chosen.

For example, let us suppose that Mary, Peter, Tom, Anne and Bob were the guessers and Eileen was the selector.

- Mary guessed the right answer and her definition fooled one person. Her score is 3 + 2 for a total of 5.
- Peter's definition fooled two people. His score is 2 + 2 for a total of 4.
- Tom guessed the right answer but fooled nobody. His score is 3.
- Anne guessed wrong and fooled nobody. Her score is 0.
- Bob guessed wrong and fooled one person. His score is 2.
- Eileen's definition from the dictionary fooled three people. Her score is 3.

By the way, it's a good idea to try to allow each member of the group to become selector once. Also, to speed up the game, the order of selectors should be agreed upon in advance. Thus, while the first selector is deciphering handwriting and mixing the papers, the second selector can be choosing a word from the dictionary. To be fair, selectors should not pick proper names, foreign words—including British dialect—or Scottish or obsolete words.

In the first example given above, all the people seemed to take the game seriously. To add to the fun, the host might play the role of jester and write outlandish or punny definitions that will fool nobody but will evoke roars of laughter. For example, consider Bill Slattery—an author who lives in Rhode Island. Bill's interest in solving crossword puzzles led to our friendship. A few years ago, he hosted a party attended by me and several other word lovers. I introduced Fictionary and a member of the group chose the word *hicatee* from *Webster's Third New International Dictionary*. As it turned out, both Bill and I independently decided to create ridiculous definitions. Here are the results:

1. Indian moccasin
2. sea mammal ranging from Florida to Patagonia
3. animal found in the Australian Outback
4. what's hicatee to me or me to hicatee
5. a West Indian freshwater tortoise
6. area on a rural golf course
7. an Irish regimental soldier of the fifteenth century
8. species of hickory in southern United States

Now, of course, you can guess that #4 and #6 are just plain jokes. Who wrote them? Well, I was the perpetrator of #6 and Bill concocted #4, which drew the most roars of appreciation from a group familiar with Shakespeare. You may remember Hamlet's soliloquy about the chief of the actors whom he has hired to trap his cruel uncle into admission that he had murdered Hamlet's father. The prince says: "What's Hecuba to him or he to Hecuba, That he should weep for her?" Unfortunately Bill mixed up Hecuba (wife of Priam) with Hecate (goddess of witchcraft, etc.). But what the heck, he hit the correct initial syllable along with the funny bones of his guests. What was the correct answer? See page 211.

Later that evening, a selector chose the word *ridotto*. Not wishing to compete with Bill's predilection for humor, I opted for a serious definition. Here are the entries:

1. laughable, Italian style
2. a Mediterranean dagger used for ceremonial occasions
3. an editor or translator of foreign works
4. a recounting, as in census taking
5. swiftly, in music
6. a fortification set up in advance of the front line
7. public entertainment consisting of music and dancing
8. slogan adopted by opponents of a Roman emperor

Naturally, you know that #8 is intended to sell the group a "Bill" of goodies. But look at those other seven definitions! If you have never encountered *ridotto* in your life, you should have a hard time picking out the correct answer.

You are referred to page 211 for the solution. Also, please note that this game is not suited to a group of high-school dropouts.

About twelve years ago, I played Fictionary with Margaret Farrar, Will Weng, Harriett Wilson (chief *New York Times* crossword-puzzles proofer) and my late wife, Jean. Guess who won? No, it wasn't Mrs. Farrar or her successor, nor was it Ms. Wilson. Jean's clever clues trapped us all. Yours truly came in last.

When my turn as selector came, I chose *deipnosophist*. Here are the entries:

1. an outstanding college student
2. one skilled in the art of table talk
3. an expert in infants' clothing
4. a believer in the transmutation of gods and beasts
5. a plastic surgeon

What's the correct definition? See page 211.

If the above descriptions have aroused your interest, and if you and your friends wish to speed up the process of picking out words from the dictionary, I recommend the following forty choices, all of which can be found in such outstanding lexicons as: *Webster's Third New International Dictionary, Random House Dictionary, Webster's New World Dictionary* and *American Heritage Dictionary.*

ataraxia	fimbriate	lugger	triturate
auscultation	gaselier	myrmecology	usquebaugh
benthos	grisaille	nankeen	ustulate
bolometer	hubris	objurgate	valgus
bombazine	huckaback	picul	williwaw
calendula	innervate	pyretic	xanthous
cavetto	jacinth	quodlibet	yamen
demulcent	jactation	recusant	yataghan
euphorbia	koto	sequacious	zareba
fastigiate	lovage	talipot	zarf

On page 211, you will find definitions for the above words. My source in this case was *Webster's New World Dictionary.*

FICTIONARY VARIATIONS: Last Lines

My daughter Merryl and I have invented two variations of Fictionary. Both involve writing the last line of a literary work, either prose or poetry. With regard to prose, the selector reads the last paragraph of a novel or short story but omits the last sentence. Then members of the group finish the paragraph. The selector collects the slips of paper, mixes them up with the slip containing the author's last sentence. Finally, the members of the group vote separately in an effort to choose the correct answer.

Here are three examples; the first is from W. Somerset Maugham's *Of Human Bondage:*

> "He smiled and took her hand and pressed it. They got up and walked out of the gallery. They stood for a moment at the balustrade and looked at Trafalgar Square."

The next is from *Manhattan Transfer,* by John Dos Passos:

> " 'Say will you give a lift?' he asks the redhaired man at the wheel.
> " 'How fur ye goin?' "

The third example is from John F. Kennedy's *Profiles in Courage:*

> "The stories of past courage can define that ingredient—they can teach, they can offer hope, they can provide inspiration. But they can't supply courage itself."

The last line of each of the above three works of prose appears on page 211.

The poetry game can be played with verses that may or may not rhyme. Here are two examples; the first is from "Revelation," a poem by Robert Frost:

> We make ourselves a place apart
>   Behind light words that tease and flout,
> But oh, the agitated heart

The next is from a nonrhyming poem by William Butler Yeats:

> Land of Heart's Desire
> Where beauty has no ebb, decay no flood,

The last line of each of the above stanzas appears on page 212. Incidentally, in the prose and poetry variations of Fictionary, the host may wish to save time by duplicating in advance enough copies for all the guests. In such cases, since the host is the only selector, he does not participate in the competition for points.

CHARADES

Charades is one of the most popular party games involving words. There are all kinds of ways to play the game. Some groups do not allow the charader to speak at all and they develop various codes and signals with their fingers and hands. An oft-used version is to allow some silent signals and no speaking on the part of the charader. For example, it should be established in advance that the charader's *first* finger signal should be preceded by drawing a *W* in the air. Then if two fingers are raised, the item to be guessed contains two words. Three fingers would equal three words, etc.

Also it should be agreed that the charader's second signal indicates which word will be concentrated on if multiple words are in the answer. For instance, if *Lucille Ball* is the name to be conveyed and the charader wants to work on *Ball*, he or she again holds up two fingers.

Concentration on syllables is performed as follows. The charader traces an *S* in the air and then indicates by fingers which syllable will be acted out. In this sophisticated pantomime, the charaders indicate that rhymes are called for by pulling their own ears or cupping their ears with their hands. Thus, if a charader wishes to tell the group that a rhyme for *Ball* is being described, he or she might do the ear bit and then touch a wall in the room.

My own favorite way to play is to eliminate all such signals and let the charader call them out. For instance, in the Lucille Ball case, the charader says: "Two words. First word is two syllables. Second word is one syllable. Let's try a rhyme for the second word." He or she then touches the wall, and members of the group shout out rhymes for *wall* until finally *Ball* is called and the charader either says yes or nods.

Admittedly, the above method offends the purists who prefer to make the charader into a perfect pantomimist, but for ordinary parties in which several members of the group have never played Charades, I think it is wise to get rid of all the folderol.

Here's an important point. Before the game begins, the rules should be outlined and the group should be divided into two teams. Also, the category for the charaders should be decided upon. Some possible categories are:

1. Famous people in general
2. Movie stars
3. Names of novels
4. Well-known geographic places
5. Fictional characters
6. Famous writers

The list could go on and on, but it's important that it not be too narrow or too esoteric.

Now, let us say that all members of the group decide on category #1 and two teams are designated—possibly by the host or by drawing lots. The next step is for the teams to meet in separate rooms and make their lists of famous people. The names of these celebrities, past or present, are then written on separate slips of paper. Fairness is definitely required at this point. Teams should choose names that are really renowned—not those that are only somewhat familiar. For example, Nicholas Rowe was a poet laureate of England in 1715, but how many people would know his name? In my own experience, the best charades lists have been prepared by the host and hostess in advance and they have acted as referees during the game.

Here are two lists of famous people prepared a few years ago by a splendid host and hostess whose choices lent themselves to Charades.

TEAM A	TEAM B
Caesar	Washington
Homer	Marilyn Monroe
Arnold Palmer	Babe Ruth
F. D. Roosevelt	William Faulkner

Note that the charaders must always perform for their own team.

Presented with *Washington,* my team member pretended she was scrubbing clothes for the first two syllables and then acted out a situation in which she was carrying a heavy weight.

When *Caesar* was given to a male member of Team B, he immediately grabbed the loveliest woman at the party and his team soon got the point—(seize her!).

Ms. *Monroe* was my responsibility. I called out the second syllable of the second word and pretended to be rowing a boat. One of the brighter members of my team caught on. At first she yelled ''President Monroe,'' but my negative reply prompted her to think twice.

Homer came easily to our opponents. The charader pretended he was at the plate (using a pencil as a bat!); with hands over his eyebrows he simulated watching the ball go out of the park.

Babe Ruth proved to be a bit difficult for our team. The charader acted as if she were cradling an infant in her arms. We guessed ''baby'' and when she switched to the second word by calling out a rhyme, she pointed to one of her teeth!

Palmer caused our opponents no trouble. Their man merely pointed to the palm of his hand and then pretended to swing at a golf ball (à la Johnny Carson).

Faulkner took only a few seconds for our team because the charader ran out into the kitchen and came back with a fork.

As for *Roosevelt,* a clever woman combined rhymes with *nose* and *belt.* When she grabbed at my pants holder-upper, everybody got a laugh.

There are numerous ways to keep score. My preference is to set a time limit for each charade. Three minutes seems reasonable. If the group guesses the answer during the first minute, 3 points are awarded. If it takes them two minutes, then their score is 2, and if they catch on during the third minute, they receive only 1 point. Of course, if they fail, they get a score of 0.

In the game mentioned above, our host was the timer and our hostess recorded the points. At the end, each member of the winning team received a pocket notebook.

ANTI-MATCH GAME

Back in 1984, Will Shortz organized a luncheon in New York City in honor of Margaret Farrar. About a hundred crossword-puzzle editors and constructors attended that gala event. Toward the end of the party a young editor-constructor named Mike Shenk introduced a game that he had invented, and it caused a great deal of hilarity. He called it the Anti-Match Game.

Mr. Shenk called out ten commands and asked us to write down our answer each time, but to try to give an answer that would not be repeated by anyone else. However, he warned us that sometimes in seeking to be unique we might fall into a trap, because others would be on the same wavelength.

To give an example, suppose that the leader's order is: "Name a flower beginning with the letter *r*." Immediately *rose* pops up in your mind. You realize that the same blossom will probably occur to the others, and so you write *rhododendron*. Lo and behold, later you discover that many others had chosen *rhododendron*, while only one person had stuck to *rose!*

Here's a list of ten commands, some of which are Mr. Shenk's.

1. Name a state in the U.S.A. that ends in *A*
2. Name a color of the spectrum
3. Name a European capital
4. Pick a number from 1 to 10, inclusive
5. Name an object in this room
6. Name a movie star, dead or alive, whose first name is Peter or Paul
7. Name one of the continents
8. Name a U.S. president since Coolidge
9. Name an instrument in an orchestra
10. Name a N.Y.C. street that runs north and south and has the word Avenue as part of its title

Please note that the commands in this game are as simple as possible. The idea is not to discover who is the brightest or most informed person in the group, but who is lucky or shrewd enough to choose answers that others have either discarded or have not thought of.

Here's the scoring system. If no one else chose the same answer as you for an individual item, you earn a 0. If one other person's answer is identical with yours, you both get 1 point. If three people pick the same answer, all three get 2 points each, etc., etc. The person with the *lowest* score for all ten items is the winner.

One other aspect of scoring needs to be mentioned. If a person gives a wrong answer, his or her score for that item is 3 points. For example, if Milan is given by someone as a capital for item #3, that person gets 3 points.

If you are about to host a party, try the above ten commands, but the group will probably want an encore; hence, I suggest that you prepare another ten in advance. Remember to keep them as simple as possible.

CATEGORIES

Categories is a fascinating game. Let us say that five people are playing it. Each is given a pencil and a blank sheet (about the size of typing paper) and something with a hard surface to work on. Next, all members of the group draw a figure containing twenty-five boxes. Here's an example:

The members of the group then take turns calling out categories. These are placed at the left of the square. Next, each person calls out a letter of the alphabet. These are placed atop the square. At this point all the squares might look like this:

	C	S	T	R	A
fish					
flowers					
statesmen					
actresses					
countries					

A time limit is then set. The larger the group, the longer the time limit should be. For a group of five, a limit of ten minutes is probably reasonable.

Using the above example, I have just timed myself and this is the result:

	C	S	T	R	A
fish	cod	shad	trout	rudd	
flowers	columbine	snapdragon	tulip	rose	aster
statesmen	Churchill	Stevenson	Tyler	Roosevelt	Attlee
actresses	Colbert	Swanson		Rogers	Albright
countries	Chile	Sweden	Thailand	Rumania	Albania

(Note that I could not think of a fish beginning with *A*, nor could I name an actress whose surname starts with *T*. For those two items I receive a 0.)

Now the fun really begins! As in Mr. Shenk's game, the aim is to try to be different. Starting with the person who chose the "fish" category, the entries in those five boxes going across are called out one by one.

Let us say that in the corner where I wrote *cod*, two other persons had that same fish. A fourth member had entered *croaker* and the last person had written *carp*.

Croaker and *carp* each receive 5 points because neither fish was used by anyone else. The other two people and I receive only 3 points apiece because of the repetition.

Here's a summary of the scoring for a group of five people:

Entry not used by anyone else	5 points
Entry used by one other person	4 points
Entry used by two others	3 points
Entry used by three others	2 points
Entry used by everybody	1 point
No entry	0 points

Incidentally, as the entries are called out, each person writes his or her own score in the appropriate box. For instance, I would write 3 next to *cod* on my sheet. The maximum for each box should match the number of players. For example, if seven persons were in the above game, *croaker* and *carp* would each earn 7 points. *Cod* would get 5 points. At the end, all players add up their points and a winner is declared.

One of the best features of Categories is that the choices of classifications are so numerous. Off the top of my head, here is a list of twenty possibilities:

trees	famous athletes
cars	rivers and lakes
magazines	four-legged animals
great novels	parts of the body
famous writers	clothing
capitals	occupations
parts of a house	famous musicians
furniture	musical instruments
famous artists	famous comedians
TV programs	birds

The key to a good game of Categories is to insist that the choices of classifications not be narrow, esoteric or completely unfamiliar to many in the group. The Seven Wonders of the World is not broad enough and, besides, it would be an unusual group that could recall all of them. Also, in one game that I played last year, a smart aleck tried to give members of the Chicago Bears as his category. The group vetoed him. But remember that vetoes should be democratic. One or two objections are not enough. The majority should rule.

MISHMASH

The boxes in the previous game reminded me of another pastime that my late wife and I enjoyed for many years. We called it Mishmash because the outcome was often a hodgepodge of letters that made no sense, along with some legitimate words.

If three or more people play Mishmash, each should draw a 7 × 7 square containing forty-nine boxes. If only two people participate, the square should be 5 × 5 and contain only twenty-five boxes.

The rules are simple. The players draw lots to see who goes first. Then the first player calls out a letter which *everybody* enters into any box in the grid. Once a letter has been entered, it may not be erased or shifted to another box. In fact, it is preferable to use pens in this game.

The object of Mishmash is to place as many words as you can into the grid and to try for long words here and there, because the long ones score far more points than the small ones.

After Player 1 has called out a letter and *everybody* has entered it, Player 2 calls out a letter which all participants must enter somewhere. The play continues until every box contains a letter.

Now the players circle the words they have managed to create, across and down, and add up their scores. If three or more players are involved, the scoring is as follows:

7-letter word	20 points
6-letter word	15 points
5-letter word	10 points
4-letter word	7 points
3-letter word	4 points
2-letter word	2 points

(If only two players participate, merely disregard the scores for 7-letter words and 6-letter words, because the 5 × 5 grid allows a maximum of only five letters.) The rules that I favor do not allow overlapping. Thus, if a player has created PANT, only 7 points are awarded. He or she cannot also claim PA, PAN, AN and ANT. Moreover, my strict rules do not allow points for diagonal entries or backwards entries (bottom to top or right to left), because it gets too confusing. But to each his own; if such entries are your cup of tea, go ahead.

Mishmash involves strategies, as you will see the longer you play the game. For example, if Player 1 calls *V*, it would be silly to place that letter in the bottom-right corner because so few words end in *V*. Again, if *J* is the first letter called, it might be wise to place it in the upper-left corner because that letter probably has more chance as the start of a word than somewhere else. Certainly, it does not belong at the end. The only words I can think of that end in *J* are RAJ and HAJJ. Another strategy is to call out consonants and hope that some weaker opponent will settle for a vowel. By the way, in this game (as in many others), proper names, obsolete words, abbreviations, foreign words, etc., are not scored.

Have fun with Mishmash! It's a great game to play with a partner on a plane trip, partly because it takes up so little space.

HANKY-PANKY

The next game, one that I have always enjoyed, has many names. Some call it Hanky-Panky; others prefer Lazy-Daisy, Stinky-Pinky or even Stink-Pink. It depends on what part of the country you live in.

At any rate, the object of the game is to create an appropriate rhyme in response to a clue. For example, a player gives the following clue: "Multiplying in a warren." Another player calls out, "Rabbits' habits."

This game can be played for points (1 point for each correct guess) or just for fun. In any case, it's a great party game, and I like it especially because it does not require paper and pencil. All you need is a sense of rhyme and a little brainpower.

Here are some Hanky-Panky clues that come to mind. The answers appear on page 212.

1. Inane Easter flower
2. Oriental joints
3. Siberian with a dog team
4. Stirring of mollusks
5. Dumb Eros
6. Serene Grange
7. Spoiled Alabama crop
8. More jazzy sailing boat
9. Chief of police
10. Maintenance man

Some more rigorous devotees of this game require that the clue reveal the number of syllables in both words of the answer. For example, "Area in Cambridge" should be described as a Hanky-Pank or Stinky-Pink because the answer (*Harvard Yard*) has only one syllable in the second word. To give another example, "Amazon's censorship" would be described as a Hank-Pank or Stink-Pink because both parts of the answer (*Man ban*) contain only one syllable.

I personally like this stricture, but *de gustibus non est disputandum*. In non-Latin words: Suit your own taste, and I won't quarrel with you. The important thing is to set the rules in advance and then have fun.

WHAT WOULD YOU BE DOING?

Here's a change of pace that requires an outrageous sense of humor, imagination, and a way with words rather than a knowledge of words. This party game is called What Would You Be Doing?

The host distributes paper and pencils to the guests. Then he tells them: "I'm going to ask you one question. When you answer it, don't tell me the truth. Let your pipe dreams and daydreams take over. The most outlandish and ridiculous reply will be the winner."

Then the host asks, "What would you be doing if you were not here tonight?"

I played this game with some friends in Massachusetts, and here are some of the answers:

1. I'd be at the White House advising the President on what to do about the national debt. I put him on hold in order to attend this party.
2. As head of the Flounder-Cleaning Club in Duxbury, I would be demonstrating the art of scaling.
3. I'd be at my usual post in Massachusetts General Hospital, pretending I'm a certified surgeon, and I'd be removing the appendix from some trusting soul.
4. I'd be telling Joan Collins it's all over between us, and she would be begging me to give her one more chance.
5. I would be continuing my efforts to organize a women's basketball team that would eventually challenge the Celtics.
6. I would be finishing the last chapter of my "Great American Novel."

My answer is one of the above. Can you guess it? By the way, it was not voted the winner by the group. Can you pick the winner? The results are listed on page 212.

MIXED-UP MELODIES

The following game can be played by you alone, or you can copy it, make carbons and distribute it at a party. It's my original creation, and I must confess it's full of puns. If you use it at a party, I suggest that soft music be played in the background.

The title of the game is Mixed-Up Melodies, and it's merely a matching test. The one who finishes first with all correct answers is the winner. Don't forget to have a prize on hand. (May I suggest this book as a possible award? Well, okay, maybe a cassette would be a better choice.)

Here's a sample game of Mixed-Up Melodies. Match the clues in the first list with the answers in the second list by placing the correct letter in the blank provided at the left.

1. _____ Song to a Surrealist   A. Danzig in the Dark
2. _____ Song for Donald Duck   B. The Gandhi Man
3. _____ Women's Lib Song   C. If I Had My Weigh
4. _____ Evening Song in Poland   D. Big Horse I Love You
5. _____ Song for Brynhild   E. After the Bawl
6. _____ Song of India   F. Battle Him
7. _____ Racetrack Song   G. Hello, Dali
8. _____ Nose-blowing Song   H. The Old Gray Mayor
9. _____ Song for the Obese   I. Sigurd Love
10. _____ Song for Koch's Predecessor   J. Waddle I Do

The correct matches can be found on page 212.

TWENTY QUESTIONS

Old-timers who enjoyed radio programs in pretelevision days will remember: "Is it bigger than a breadbox?" That query was often asked in "Twenty Questions" from 1946 to 1954. The Van Deventer family brought the game to the airwaves, but it was not exactly their invention. Prior to their popularization of the game, folks had been playing Animal-Mineral-Vegetable for many years. One of the chief contributions of the Van Deventers was that they taught lots of people how to zero in on the answer through an orderly sequence of questions.

In case you are unfamiliar with Twenty Questions, the game starts when a member of the group secretly writes down a person, fictional character, place or thing. Then the others take turns asking questions that ideally can be answered by a *yes* or a *no*.

Let's start with an easy one. The leader writes down *John F. Kennedy*. Questions and answers might go like this:

QUESTION	ANSWER
1. Is it animal?	Yes
2. Is it fictional?	No
3. Is it a human being?	Yes
4. Is it female?	No
5. Is he living?	No
6. Was he American?	Yes
7. Did he live in this century?	Yes
8. Was he famous in one of the arts?	No
9. Was he a politician or a statesman?	Yes
10. Was he a U.S. president?	Yes
11. Was he a president before FDR?	No
12. Was he assassinated?	Yes
13. Was it JFK?	Yes

In the above case, the correct answer was obtained on the thirteenth try. The object of the game is to guess the answer on or before the twentieth question—hence the title.

Note the importance of question #2. In the "animal" category, it helps to establish immediately whether the individual is real or fictional.

Question #3 eliminated all beasts, reptiles, birds, etc., and question #4 established the sex. Questions #5, #6, and #7 further narrowed the field until, finally, it was easy to reach the right answer.

Let's examine another example in a different category. The answer is, *The New York Times*.

QUESTION	ANSWER
1. Is it animal?	No
2. Is it mineral?	No
3. Is it a plant?	No
4. Is it derived from a plant?	Yes
5. Is it a book or magazine?	No
6. Is it a newspaper?	Yes
7. Is it still being published?	Yes
8. Is it an American newspaper?	Yes
9. Is it a New York newspaper?	Yes
10. Is it published in the morning?	Yes
11. Is it a tabloid?	No
12. Does it contain a crossword puzzle?	Yes
13. Is it the *New York Times?*	Yes

Questions #1 and #2 reduced the category to "vegetable." Question #4 put the group on the right track because wood is the ultimate source of paper.

Note how carefully the group homed in on the right answer. Question #8 eliminated all foreign newspapers such as the London *Times.* Question #10 eliminated the *New York Post,* and question #11 excluded the *Daily News.* Finally, at question #12 the *Wall Street Journal* was put out of the running because it has no crossword puzzle.

In that connection, it behooves the guessers not to jump the gun when they get close. If the *Wall Street Journal* had been the correct answer, and at question #12 a member of the group had blurted out, "Is it *The New York Times?*" the leader would have won the game. The only time a guesser should take a wild stab is when question #20 is reached.

Here's another example, but this one contains two common problems in Twenty Questions. The leader picks Fulton's *Clermont,* the famous steamboat. The initial problem is that, contrary to popular opinion, the *Clermont* was not the first steamboat, but it was the first to promise a fair profit to its owners. If the leader knows that fact but the members of the group do not (or vice versa), confusion can reign. In other words, care must be taken in the choice of the items to be guessed. Of greatest importance is that the leader should have more than a vague knowledge of the subject.

For example, in a game in which I recently participated, the leader had chosen Nero. When asked if the person lived in the B.C. period, he responded, "Yes." However, Nero was born in A.D. 38 and died during A.D. 68.

The second problem about the *Clermont* is that it belongs to two categories— "vegetable" because of the wood and "mineral" because of the metal boilers.

In such a case, fairness to the group is needed. Here's the best way out:

QUESTION	ANSWER
1. Is it animal?	No
2. Is it mineral?	Partly

The purer method is for the leader to say yes to question #2 and for the next member of the group to ask if it's wholly mineral. Otherwise, they will probably end up with the *Monitor* or the *Merrimac*.

Similarly, if a Model-T Ford is chosen, the categories are probably "animal" (because of the leather), "mineral" (because of the metal), and "vegetable" (because of the rubber tires).

Yes, Twenty Questions can lead to complications and controversy, but it's one of my favorites for three reasons:

1. It makes you think carefully and logically.
2. It doesn't require paper and pencils for the group.
3. It can be played anywhere—in a car, at a picnic, etc.

Here are twenty-one uncomplicated choices for you to consider as selections for a Twenty Questions party:

ANIMAL
any U.S. president
Rhett Butler
King Kong
Queen Victoria
Bambi
Napoleon
Loch Ness monster

MINERAL
penny, dime or quarter
wedding ring
the Plymouth Rock
sculptures on Mount Rushmore
pebbles in Pebble Beach (California)
mirror in the Snow White tale
golden apple thrown by Eris

VEGETABLE
Sherwood Forest
rose in Rose Bowl Pageant
Dutchman's sabot
Yankee Stadium infield
Gandhi's dhoti
President's Oval Office chair
Mom's apple pie

BOTTICELLI

Botticelli is a game that I have played often at parties in the Northeast. I don't know what it's called elsewhere, and I haven't the foggiest notion as to why it bears the name of an Italian painter. He really seems irrelevant unless when the game originated it was confined to the guessing of artists' names.

Anyway, Botticelli is a fine party game that requires no paper or pencils. Like Twenty Questions and other brainteasers, it can be played while riding in a car or sitting around at a barbecue.

Here's how the game goes. Susan is chosen to lead, and after cogitation she gives the initials of a well-known person or fictional character. Now let us suppose that she chooses *Minnie Mouse.* Let us also assume that Andy, Barbara, Carl and Donna are the guessers.

Andy is thinking of *Marilyn Monroe.* He must not ask a direct question because if he is wrong, he is eliminated from that round of the game. Hence, Andy asks: "Are you a former blonde movie star?"

Susan must now know to whom Andy is referring. She says, "No, I am not Marilyn Monroe."

Now it is Barbara's turn. She is thinking of *Mary Martin,* and so she asks, "Did you ever play Peter Pan?"

Her easy question gives it away, and Susan replies, "No, I am not Mary Martin."

Carl comes up next. Feeling sure that *Mickey Mantle* is the right answer, he asks, "Are you a former Yankee slugger?"

Susan happens to know nothing about baseball, so takes a wild guess and says, "No, I am not Monty Murphy."

Because she has missed, Carl now has a chance to ask a general question that requires a *yes* or *no.* He inquires, "Are you a fictional character?" and Susan must give him a positive response.

The questioning now shifts to Donna. Knowing that M.M. is fictional, she asks, "Are you the hero of a Disney film?"

Susan replies, "No, I am not Mickey Mouse."

Andy's second turn comes up next. He has had enough evidence to ask, "Are you the mate of Mickey Mouse?"

The game is over, and Andy wins a point, thanks to Donna. Since he has triumphed, he also gets the chance to become the leader.

Note: Players must take turns asking questions. If Donna's excellent lead had caused Barbara or Carl to ascertain the correct answer, he or she must remain mute because it is Andy's turn.

It is not easy to summarize the rules for Botticelli, but I will try.

1. The leader must give the initials of a *really famous* person or fictional character that most members of the group can be expected to know.
2. Players take turns asking questions.
3. When a player makes the wrong guess but has the correct initials, the leader must be able to identify the player's choice.
4. If the leader does identify the player's wrong choice, the next member of the group becomes the guesser.
5. If the leader is unable to identify a player's choice, that player is allowed to ask a general question that will help to zero in on the name the leader has in mind. Carl's question in the above example was excellent because it established that the answer was a fictional character. Other good questions at this point are:

   Are you living?
   Are you a male?
   Are you connected with movies or TV?
   Are you a sports figure?
   Are you in politics or government?

6. Once the leader has been stumped (as Susan was by Carl's initial question about Mickey Mantle), and the questioner is allowed to ask a *general* question requiring a *yes* or *no,* the door has been opened.
7. A time period should be set. If it expires, the leader is the winner of that round and gets 1 point. The next person in line then becomes the leader.

It should be noted that two initials are usually required in Botticelli. Using one initial (as for Homer or Horace) is too easy or too hard, and three initials are usually too simple. For example:

MTM	Mary Tyler Moore
WSM	W. Somerset Maugham
TSE	T. S. Eliot
JFK	You know who!

I urge you to peruse the above illustration and rules for Botticelli. After you grasp the idea completely, you can undertake a trial run with your friends. Once they catch on, lots of fun lies ahead!

SCRIBBLE / JOTTO

The next game is one for which I have two different names. The variation, which I like better, was called Scribble by a Massachusetts friend who taught me how to play it. An offspring, if I recall correctly, was called Jotto by some commercial company.

In any case, Scribble has produced many hours of pleasure for me and my family. At this point, please permit me to become personal. For almost two decades, my late wife and I lived in New Jersey and owned a summer cottage near Cape Cod. The trip between the two in our car consumed about 240 miles and over five hours. During the long journey we would play various games with our little children, who sat in the back. Some games involved spotting license plates of the various states and Canada. Others were built around number combinations on the licenses. But the game we enjoyed most was Scribble, and I think it helped to develop the children's interest in words.

Since Gary was the youngest, he was given the shortest and easiest words to guess. His were the three-letter words, Merryl got fours. Jean had to guess five-letter words and sixes were reserved for me.

Here's how it works. Let us say that it's Gary's turn to guess, and I decide secretly that *cap* is the word.

>Gary: Is it *rat?*
>Dad: One point.
>Gary: Is it *cat?*
>Dad: Two points!
>Gary: Is it *car?*
>Dad: Still two points.
>Gary: Is it *cap?*
>Dad: That's it! Three points!

In the above example, Gary received 1 point for the *a* in *rat* because he had guessed the right letter in the right spot. *Cat* and *car* earned him 2 points because two of the three letters were correct and were in their proper places.

Here's another example. Jean secretly picks *rain* as the word for Merryl to guess. Merryl's calls are as follows:

>1. walk   1 point (for the *a*)
>2. talk   1 point (for the *a*)

3. tail   2 points (for the *a, i*)
4. hail   2 points (for the *a, i*)
5. rail   3 points (for the *r, a, i*)
6. raid   3 points (for the *r, a, i*)
7. rain   4 points

In the above case, suppose that Merryl's first guess had been *liar*. She would get no points even though three of the letters are the same as those in *rain*. The reason is that those three letters are in the wrong spots. Now if she changes *liar* to *lair,* she gets 2 points for the *a, i* in the middle.

Scribble requires deduction. Using *rain* as the example again, suppose Merryl's first call was *rope,* for which she would receive 1 point. Next she calls *hope* and receives no points. The loss of the point should tell her that the word in question must begin with *r*. She also should realize that her last three letters are either hopelessly wrong or are in the wrong spots.

For the average person, four-letter words are the best to start with. After gaining experience and facility, some may wish to "graduate" to five-letter words. I personally prefer the challenge of seven-letter words.

Simplified scoring is 1 point for each word correctly guessed. Also, the maximum is twenty calls, and if the guesser exceeds that limit, the person who posed the word gets 1 point. Needless to say, players take turns guessing.

Jotto is a bit harder than Scribble because deduction is slightly more complicated. In this game the guesser gets points for letters, even though they are in the wrong spots. For example, let us go back to *rain*. If Merryl had guessed *liar,* she would have received 3 points for the *r,* the *i,* and the *a,* even though they are in the wrong spots.

Now Merryl tries *nail* and still gets 3 points, even though she traded an *r* for an *n*. Next she guesses *rail* and again gets her 3. At this point, you can see why Jotto becomes mind-boggling. Merryl must be astute enough to see that both the *n* and the *r* must be kept and that she picked up the other 2 points for *a, i*. Her only choice, if she has thought it through, is *rain*.

Here's a Jotto example in which a five-letter word was to be guessed by me. The secret word was *field*. My guesses and my reasoning are as follows:

1. story   0 points (Anything to get started.)
2. store   1 point (Hooray, there's an *e* in the word!)
3. stage   1 point (I'm getting nowhere.)

4. stale   2 points (Good! Now I know that *l* is in it.)
5. lemon   2 points (Well, I've eliminated *m, o, n* in addition to *s, t, r, y, a* and *g*.)
6. alien   3 points (It has to be the *i* because *n* and *a* are no good.)
7. glide   4 points (It must be the *d* because *g* gave me no points for *stage*. Now I have *l, i, d, e*. What word has all those letters?)
8. yield   4 points (That was stupid! I already knew that *y* was no good.)
9. field   5 points (Voilà!)

Note that changing one letter at a time is usually good strategy in either Scribble or Jotto, but if you keep getting a zero score, you might want to switch to an entirely new word that uses none of the letters in your original guess.

Many people prefer to use paper and pencil for these two games. They write down the letters that have already been eliminated, and in a separate place they record the letters that have clicked.

I'll never forget the time that my second wife, Annrea, tricked me on *zebra* in a Scribble game. I had reached the point where I knew that the word ended in *ebra*. Naturally, I went through the alphabet aloud to find that first letter. When I came to *debra*, I turned to Annrea and said, "Foul! You should know that proper names are not allowed."

She smiled. "No, it's not *Debra*."

"Okay, I'll keep going. *febra, gebra, hebra, jebra* . . .''

When I came to the end of the alphabet, Debra was still in my mind. Hence, I called out *zebra* with a short *e*, pronouncing it as if it were *zebbra*.

"I give up," I said. "You must have picked a word I never heard of."

"But you had it," she answered. "It's *zebra*—pronounced *zeebra!*"

You can imagine my embarrassment. *Debra* and my wife had trapped me.

On another occasion, Annrea beat me with *phlox*. I had the first three letters but couldn't think of any word that began with *p-h-l*. My excuse is that I was driving the car on a crowded highway.

Esoteric words are taboo in Scribble or Jotto, but here are some familiar four-letter words that will probably cause trouble for the guesser. Note that not one of the words repeats the same letter. I have learned from experience that words such as *fife, jazz,* and *kick* cause complications.

adze	halo	myth	thou
axle	hazy	nick	toga
buck	iota	oxen	tyro
coma	jinx	phew	whiz
czar	junk	pyre	wick
debt	kiln	quip	xray
exit	lazy	quiz	yoga
faze	lynx	rove	zero
flax	lyre	sexy	zinc
gnaw	mewl	taxi	

Note, also, that plurals ending in *s* should not be used.

Now here are some five-letter stumpers.

azure	gnash	lingo	ritzy
banjo	hydra	moxie	squid
bayou	hyena	nifty	toque
calyx	index	omega	toxic
dozen	julep	phlox	ultra
enjoy	jumbo	pique	viola
extol	jumpy	psalm	waxen
flaky	ketch	quasi	yacht
gizmo	knarl	quick	zebra

GHOST

Ghost is another old-fashioned game that can be played anywhere and doesn't require paper and pencil. Its continuous popularity probably results from the fact that it is so simple to play.

In case you are one of the few people who have never played Ghost, here's an outline.

1. Any number can play.
2. The object of the game is *not* to form a word.
3. When a person forms a word, he or she becomes a *G*. If the same person forms another word in a subsequent round, he or she is a *G-H*. The game continues until one player finally becomes a *G-H-O-S-T*.
4. Players take turns starting each round by calling out one letter of the alphabet. Successive players then call letters to follow the first one.
5. Each time a player calls a letter, he or she must have a word in mind. If the letter that is called happens to stump the next player, that person may issue a challenge. At that point, if the challenged player had no word in mind or had misspelled a word or had broken another rule, he or she loses the round.
6. Obsolete words, proper names, foreign words and abbreviations are not allowed. Slang is usually unacceptable, but the players should decide on that matter in advance. It is also advisable to have a dictionary on hand in order to verify spelling or the existence of a word.

Here's an example of how a game might proceed. Three players are participating, and at this point Mary is winning.

Mary:	T
John:	T-W
Lola:	T-W-E
Mary:	T-W-E-L
John:	T-W-E-L-F
Lola:	T-W-E-L-F-T
Mary:	Twelfth

In this case, Mary was hoisted on her own petard. When she called T-W-E-L, she was thinking of *twelve,* which would stick Lola. But her strategy boomeranged when John called T-W-E-L-F. John, of course, wanted Mary to lose because she was ahead in the overall game.

Before going any further, I should point out that the group should decide in advance whether the creation of a two-letter word causes a person to lose the round. Personally, I favor the rule that states: The minimum must be a three-letter word. This permits more flexibility and opens up the game to legions of words that would otherwise never come up in the game.

In general, strategies are more likely to succeed when there are only two or three players. In large groups, you seldom know what will eventuate although it is possible to maneuver so that one person will be stuck rather than another.

In the previous example, suppose that six people were playing:

Mary: T
John: T-W
Lola: T-W-E
Harry: T-W-E . . .?
Nancy:
Tom:

Harry has a choice of three letters. He can call an *R* if the group has allowed slang, and if challenged, he can produce *twerp.* He can call the *L* for *twelve* or *twelfth,* or he can call an *N* for *twenty* or *twentieth.*

What about *e* for *tweet* or *tweezers?* Harry happens to be an astute player. He knows that if he calls an *e,* he has made a word. *Twee* is "a bird's sound" in unabridged dictionaries. Harry starts counting. He knows he can stick Nancy with *twerp,* but Nancy happens to be his wife and she's far behind in the game. Well, how about *twenty?* That would stick Tom! But wait! Tom is clever enough to switch to *twentieth.* Who would lose in that case? Lola. But Lola, poor girl, is already a G-H-O. Then maybe T-W-E-L is best. That would stick Mary, and she's not even a *G.*

Harry settles for an *L* and now the ball is in Nancy's court. Unfortunately she fails to see that she has a choice. Immediately she calls *V* and Tom is stuck with *twelve.*

The above shows you that "the best laid schemes o' mice and men" can "Gang aft a-gley" when playing Ghost with numerous other people.

Our friend Harry is a dangerous opponent in a one-on-one game. Recently I found out:

Gene: G
Harry: G-N
Gene: G-N-A
Harry: G-N-A-S

I thought I had him with *gnar, gnat* or *gnaw,* but he came up with *gnash.* Incidentally, crossword-puzzle fans knows that *gnar* is a word meaning "growl or snarl." I was hoping that Harry would call the *R* in the expectation of sticking me with *gnarl.*

Here's another example in which I got "Harried."

Harry: I
Gene: O (thinking of *iota*)
Harry: D

Finally, he got me with *iodine!* My advice to you is, if you ever meet a man named Harry, don't play Ghost with him unless there are lots of other players. Even then, beware and be wary of Harry!

Have you ever wondered why Ghost has never become a popular game show on TV? Well, it may be my fault. About thirty years ago, a New York City company that produces games for television called Margaret Farrar—then editor of crossword puzzles for the *New York Times.* They asked her to recommend a word expert to try out a game they were thinking about for a major network. Mrs. Farrar picked me, probably because I lived nearby. I accepted the assignment gladly because I was told that the payment would be $50 per hour. It turned out that Ghost was under consideration.

I was paired with one of the company's employees in a mock game of Ghost. He called the letter *D.* After some cogitation, I followed with an *H.* As a crossword-puzzle specialist, I had three words in mind:

1. dhobi: a laundryman in India
2. dhole: a wild dog of Asia
3. dhoti: a Hindu loincloth

All of them would cause him to lose. My opponent was immediately bewildered. He challenged me and I gave him Gandhi's *dhoti.*

Actually, he could have stuck me by calling an *A.* I would have been given a Hobson's choice—either *dharma* or *dharna.* The former means "cosmic order or law" in

India and the latter is "a method of seeking justice by sitting at the door of one's debtor or offender and fasting, to death if necessary."

However, if my opponent had called an *A*, I would have challenged him for choosing a foreign word. By the way, *dhole* and *dhoti* have been accepted into our language by lexicographers, but the other words are still at the threshold.

Now it was my turn to lead. I called an *L*. He responded with a *Y*, hoping perhaps that I would call an *N* to stick him with *lynx*, but his way out was *L-Y-N-C*, leaving me with *lynch*. Actually, he had put himself in a hole. Even if I had called an *R*, *lyrist* would have been his undoing.

I called an *M* and he succumbed to *lymph*.

Subsequently, a secret conference was held while I twiddled my thumbs. A man whom I had never met before handed me a check for $50 and said, "Thank you, Mr. Maleska. Good day."

Apparently behind closed doors the company had discovered that Ghost has a serious flaw. Words that are unfamiliar to the average American would crop up constantly unless they chose contestants with small vocabularies—and that would cause a different kind of problem.

At any rate, if you see a *ghost* on your TV set, call for a repairman!

SUPERGHOST

James Thurber and his Algonquin cronies grew tired of Ghost, and so Superghost was invented. The rules are simple enough. After a letter is called, the second player calls another letter and declares whether it goes *after* or *before* the first letter.

Here's an example:

Dorothy: H
James: P-H
Robert: O-P-H
Dorothy: H-O-P-H
James: H-O-P-H-O
Robert: H-O-P-H-O-U
Dorothy: H-O-P-H-O-U-S
James: C-H-O-P-H-O-U-S
Robert: Chophouse (he loses)

This variation of the simple game calls for more brainpower and adds lots of spice. Try it. You may like it.

HANG THE MAN

Hang the Man (also known as Hangman) is the earliest word game that I remember playing, and it's still one of my favorites. Incidentally, the title bothers some adults. When I was principal of an elementary school in New York City, I walked into one of the third-grade rooms, where a teacher was playing the game with her class. However, on the blackboard she had written, Make a Man.

The teacher explained to me that she considered the original title to be gruesome and she hated the idea of implanting lynching in the children's heads. And so, she had reversed the whole process. Any time a pupil called the correct letter, a part of the man's body was drawn on the board. And, of course, there was no scaffold!

For those few readers who have never played Hang the Man, let me review the procedure.

A piece of paper and a pencil are necessary unless you're in a classroom with a blackboard.

The leader thinks of a word or phrase or title and indicates the number of letters by drawing a series of dashes. Here are three examples:

A _ _ _ _ _ _ (for *kitten*)
B _ _ _ _ _ _ _ ' _ _ _ _ (for *batter's box*)
C _ _ _ _ _ _ _ _ (for *Peter Pan*)

Now a scaffold is drawn. It might look like this:

The guessers take turns calling out letters. When correct letters are called, the leader inserts them in the proper spots. Note that if a *T* is called in example A or B, all *T*'s are recorded. The same applies to the *P*'s and *E*'s in example C.

When the first incorrect letter is called, a head is drawn under the scaffold. When a second incorrect letter is called, a torso is drawn under the head. As play proceeds, arms and legs are added. The "man" finally looks like this:

The object of the game is for the leader to try to "hang" the guesser or guessers.

At this point, it should be noted that the participants must establish in advance how many incorrect guesses are the maximum. In the above drawing, there were six incorrect calls. Some players allow hands and feet for a total of ten incorrect calls, and others add facial features. In my opinion, six incorrect calls should be the maximum for a game involving a single word, and ten should be the limit for a long title, quotation, geographic locale, etc. If the guessers are children, as many as fourteen incorrect calls might be permitted.

It's interesting to note that the very popular television show, "Wheel of Fortune," is based on the hanging game. Over the years, participants have learned the strategy of calling the most-used consonants—S, T, R, N, L—and the ever popular vowel—E.

As for leaders' strategies in Hang the Man, it's wise to select words, phrases, etc., in which the above letters are scarce. Also, since apostrophes must be indicated, try to avoid choices that contain them. (The Scribble / Jotto list might produce a few "hangers"!)

WORD POKER

I like words and I like to play cards. That's why I invented a game called Word Poker. If you wish to play it with your friends, there is only one problem. You must acquire a supply of thin cardboard and cut out your own deck. See below under Equipment. If you don't play poker, consult any book that presents Hoyle's rules.

Also, you will need a set of chips or matches or some such—unless you would rather play for real money.

OBJECT OF THE GAME:

Each player's purpose is the same as for ordinary poker games, namely, to get the best hands and win the most chips after either a period of time or a number of rounds agreed upon in advance.

EQUIPMENT:

1. A deck of 63 playing cards, 61 of which contain a letter of the alphabet. The two extra cards ("jokers") can be used as any letter. The player who holds a joker may designate it as a certain letter at one time and as another letter later. As for the other 61, the ratio of consonants to vowels should approximate 3 to 2. For further guidance consult a Scrabble set.

2. A set of chips to be distributed before the game starts.

3. Several cards giving the precise order of winning hands (see page 52). Each player should receive one of these cards prior to the first deal. Players may wish to refer to the cards as the game progresses—and especially at the end.

START OF THE GAME:

Each player draws a card from the face-down deck. The one holding the card nearest the end of the alphabet becomes the first dealer. If a tie occurs, those who are tied should draw again.

7-CARD DRAW (two to nine players)

1. After all players ante up, the dealer gives each player seven cards, face down.
2. The player to the left of the dealer has the first chance to "open," which he or she may do regardless of the type of hand. If the player chooses not to

open, the next one to the left makes a declaration. This procedure continues until someone opens and bets whatever number of chips have been decided upon in advance.

   Note: If no one opens, all cards are collected and shuffled. Then all players ante up again, and the cards are distributed by the player to the left of the one who has just dealt.

3. After a player opens, the others may ''see'' the bet, raise it or drop out.

   Note: Players should decide upon the maximum number and amount of *raises* before the game starts.

4. As soon as all bets are in, players may discard *no more than three cards.*

5. The dealer then gives each player whatever number of cards the individual has discarded, beginning with the person on the dealer's left.

6. The ''opener'' now bets again, or checks or drops out. Play proceeds to the opener's left.

   Note: A ''check'' is a non-bet. Players who check must match the amounts bet by subsequent players, but may not raise.

7. After the betting has been completed, all players reveal their hands. The pot is then taken by the one who is declared the winner.

8. In the event of a tie, the player whose hand has a letter nearest to the end of the alphabet is the winner. If a tie *still* exists, players should refer to the card that is next nearest to the end of the alphabet.

7-CARD STUD (two to nine players)

The rules for this game are the same as those for 7-Card Draw. The procedure differs as follows:

1. After players ante up, the dealer gives each player two cards *face down,* and a third card *face up.*

2. The player at the dealer's left then bets, checks or drops out. If he or she drops out, the next player to the left has the same options. Once a bet is made, all players match it, raise or drop out.

3. Three more rounds are dealt *face up.* After *each* round, the betting takes place as described above. When a three-letter word, or better, is face up on the table, the bets may be doubled.

4. The seventh card is dealt *face down,* and the final bets are made after all players have examined their total hands.

Note: At this point, players must allow their face-up cards to remain face up on the table.

4. Players designate the combinations they wish to keep, and a winner is declared.

FOLLOW THE T (two to nine players)

This game is the same as 7-Card Stud with one exception: whenever a *T* is dealt faceup to a player, the card dealt *to the next player* becomes wild.

Since there are three *T*'s in the deck, the wild card may change as play progresses. See illustrations 1 and 2.

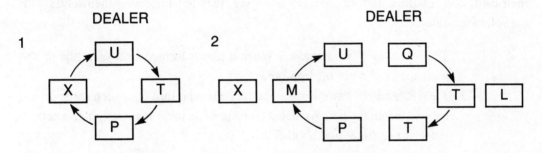

In 1, the wild card is a *P*.

In 2, the wild card is no longer a *P*. It has changed to an *M* because the player opposite the dealer has just been given another *T* faceup and the next player has received an *M*.

Note: Before this game starts, the dealer should remove the jokers.

SPIT IN THE OCEAN (two to fifteen players)

In this game, after all the players ante up, the dealer gives each player one card *face down* and places the next card *face up* in the middle of the table. That card now becomes a part of each player's hand. The player to the left of the dealer (Player 2) then has the opportunity to make the first bet.

After the betting, the dealer gives each player a second card *face down* and places the next card *face up* in the middle of the table. That card also becomes a part of each player's hand. Player 3 opens the betting in the round. Such rotation continues thereafter.

The above procedure is repeated once more so that each player now has six cards—three in his hand and three faceup on the board.

After the betting, the dealer gives each player a fourth *face-down* card and the final betting takes place. Note that each player now has *seven* cards, counting the three face-up cards.

The rules outlined in the description of 7-Card Stud also apply for Spit in the Ocean.

NO PEEK (two to nine players)

After all players ante up, the dealer gives each player seven cards, *face down*. The players then stack their cards neatly, but *are not allowed to look at the hands they have received.*

Starting with the person to the left of the dealer, players will now begin to turn over their cards one at a time. Before doing so, however, they must acquaint themselves with the following rules:

1. The jokers are "wild cards." When a player turns over a joker, he or she must match the pot or drop out.
2. *J* and *Z* are also "wild cards," but players who turn over such cards do not have to match the pot. As stated on page 47, a joker may designate a certain letter at one time, and another letter later.
3. A player who turns over an *X* must immediately drop out of the game. He or she may not look at the rest of the face-down cards until the game is over.
4. When a person turns over an *F*, the dealer must give that player an extra card from the pack. The player may place it anywhere in his or her stack.
5. As in 7-Card Draw, 7-Card Stud, etc., the letter closest to the end of the alphabet takes precedence over other letters. Thus, if the first player turns up a *T*, the next player must keep turning up cards until he or she gets a *U, V, Y,* or any wild card—*or forms a three-letter word.*
6. Each player in turn must surpass the best face-up hand on the board (see order of winning hands). As soon as this happens, he or she bets. Those who are still in the game then see the bet, raise or drop out. When a player has turned up all the cards in his or her hand and cannot surpass the best hand on the board, he or she must drop out. The person to the left then opens the betting for that round.

   Note: Each time a player completes his or her turn and is still in the game, a round of betting ensues. If the player drops out, the round of betting starts with the person to his or her left.

7. Play continues until all players except the one with the best hand have dropped out.

Additional Notes: If two players have three-letter words (or better) face-up, the one with a letter closest to the end of the alphabet surpasses the other. As for ties, let us say that Player A has CAT on the table. Player B then turns up CAT also. He or she must continue to turn up cards until Player A's hand has been surpassed.

All players should consult their extra cards as the game progresses.

Because possession of the letter *F* entitles a player to an *extra* card in this game, it must be stressed that such a player must choose only his or her best *seven* cards to compete for the best hand at the end.

6-LETTER WORDS (two to seven players)

This game is the same as 7-Card Draw, but play must continue until a player declares (after the betting) that he or she has a six-letter word or better.

If play goes to *nine rounds* the dealer gives each player a face-down card in that round.

If no player can form a six-letter word or better at the end of the ninth round, cards are collected and redealt. All players must ante up again for the "double pot."

WORD POKER LETTERS (NUMBER OF EACH LETTER REQUIRED):

A	= 6	J	= 1	T	= 3
B	= 2	K	= 1	U	= 2
C	= 2	L	= 2	V	= 1
D	= 2	M	= 2	W	= 1
E	= 7	N	= 2	X	= 1
F	= 2	O	= 5	Y	= 1
G	= 2	P	= 2	Z	= 1
H	= 2	R	= 3	Jokers	= 2
I	= 5	S	= 3		

ORDER OF WINNING HANDS (TO BE LISTED ON EXTRA CARDS)

Best hand	7-letter word
2nd best	A E I O U Y, or any 7 vowels
3rd best	6-letter word
4th best	7 consonants
5th best	A E I O U
6th best	4-letter word *and* 3-letter word
7th best	5-letter word
8th best	Two 3-letter words
9th best	4-letter word
10th best	3-letter word

CREATIVE CROSSWORDS

Millions of people who solve crossword puzzles have never had the nerve, or felt they had the skill or savvy, to construct such a puzzle. To demystify the process of construction and simultaneously provide additional fun with words, I have invented a game called Creative Crosswords. Believe it or not, in a few minutes you will be creating a genuine crossword puzzle.

But first, I must give away a secret known to all professional puzzle makers. When the horizontal words alternate consonants and vowels, the vertical words are more likely to make sense than if the horizontal words contain two or three consonants in a row. Here's an example:

R E P I N E D

A V E R A G E

P A R A G O N

Now look at all the Down words. The only one that is questionable is IRA, but if you're familiar with current investment strategies, you know about that acronym for an Individual Retirement Account. Sons of Erin will recognize it as the initials of the Irish Republican Army. Music lovers will want to define it as ''One of the Gershwins'' (Ira wrote the lyrics for many of George's scores), and avid readers will think of it as the first name of novelist Levin (he wrote *Rosemary's Baby*). At any rate, you can readily see that the consonant-vowel alternation technique has its merits. Watch for it in the next crossword puzzle that you tackle.

In the above illustration, *7-letter words* were used. Your task will be easier; you will be asked to alternate consonants and vowels in *5-letter words*. Here's a diagram that I have used several times on TV and at least twenty times in personal appearances before audiences ranging from about fifty persons to over three hundred. In each case, the members of the group had never published a crossword puzzle, but in every instance, a perfect puzzle resulted.

As indicated, this is a group game, but it can be played by a couple or by one person. Now let's play it on a solitary basis. Your first task is to fill in 4 Across with a word that alternates consonants and vowels, such as CAMEL or WATER.

Now tackle 1 Down, using the vowel that you have already placed in the second box. Next try 8 Across, using the same technique. Again, use the vowel in its second box.

Your final 5-letter word challenge is to fill in 3 Down, using the two vowels already placed in the second and fourth boxes.

Now you must concern yourself with the 3-letter words at the top, bottom and sides. If you are lucky, some of them have worked out. If not, you'll need to make a few minor changes. This happens often to professional constructors, so don't feel bad.

Lastly, the four 2-letter words must be dealt with. If you have played the game correctly, all of them contain one consonant and one vowel. Sometimes such common words as AT, TO, IN, etc., have fallen into place. At other times, look closely and use your imagination to find an abbreviation or the initials of a famous person. In a recent experience with a gaggle of advertisers for *The New York Times,* 7 Across had become TE. For a second the group felt frustrated. Then one bright copywriter yelled out, "Abbreviation for a famous American inventor!" I was glad that his light bulb had been turned on.

About seven years ago, I played the game with a charming TV hostess in Boston and her male associate. Here are the results:

	F	O	R	
B	A	K	E	S
A	T		V	I
D	E	F	E	R
	S	A	L	

Originally, they had called BAKER at 4 Across, but at the end they saw that BAKES would be a better choice. My hostess worried about 7 Across, but I assured her that Roman numerals are often used in crossword puzzles and the clue for VI could be "Six, to Caesar."

And now for the fun at your party! You have two choices:

1. Draw the 5 × 5 diagram on a large piece of cardboard and repeat the directions that I have given earlier in this section. This is a group game *just for fun* to see if the combined efforts of all present can produce an acceptable crossword puzzle.

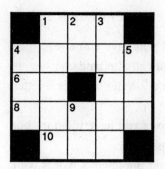
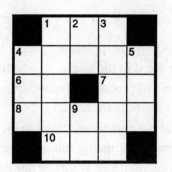

2. Duplicate copies of the diagram and give one to each person at the party. Carefully explain my directions about the consonant-vowel alternations and about the need to start with a 5-letter word, preferably 4 Across. In this instance, the person who finishes first and can defend every entry is the winner. As the host you should be ready with a prize, such as a book of crossword puzzles. (At this juncture, I will refrain from a commercial.) By the way, the explanations of the hopeful would-be winner can lead to some interesting badinage.

When Creative Crosswords is played by two persons, the couple can compete with two separate diagrams or cooperate in bringing the puzzle to a successful conclusion. In either case, they can then dream up clues and present the finished product(s) to any friends who happen to be crossword-puzzle fans.

Another version of the game is to use the daily puzzle grid in any newspaper. It can be played on a solitary basis in which you compare your score today with those of tomorrow and yesterday.

But the ideal method is for two people to vie with each other. Let's say that Mr. and Mrs. Smith are playing. Ladies first! Mrs. Smith looks at the diagram and sees a seven-letter entry. She disregards the definitions and writes in GENERAL, which fulfills the consonant-vowel alternation requirement. She gets 7 points.

Down below, Mr. Smith spots another area where he writes in PARADOX. The couple is tied.

Now Smith's wife sees a vertical section containing five boxes. The second box contains the letter A from her GENERAL. She writes in RAVEN and gets 5 points for the word, plus a bonus of 5 more points for crossing another word.

The play continues until both are stuck. Of course, unless a miracle occurs, they will not be able to complete an original crossword puzzle, but think of all the fun they will have in the meantime.

In summary, the rules and strategy for this version of Creative Crosswords are:

1. Disregard all clues for the published puzzle that you have chosen.
2. Seek the longest word in the puzzle in which you can alternate consonants and vowels. You will probably have to settle for a 7-letter word or 6-letter word unless you are brilliant or lucky.
3. Your points equal the number of letters in the boxes you have filled in, but the vowel-consonant alternating rule must be observed.
4. If you cross one of your own words or one of your opponent's words with a word alternating consonants and vowels, you receive a bonus of 5 points.
5. You may begin with a vowel and then alternate consonants and vowels. An example is ELUDE.
6. When you and your opponent cannot proceed any further, add up your respective points and declare a winner.

FIVE-BY-FIVE CROSSWORD CONTEST

Using the diagram in Creative Crosswords, each player creates his or her own puzzle, including definitions. A blank diagram plus the clues is presented by the constructor to all others in the group.

	1	2	3	
4				5
6		■	7	
8		9		
■	10			■

The usual way to score is to declare as a winner the first person to correctly complete the puzzle that he or she is solving. However, in a large group the real fun is the discussion of the various puzzles, criticisms of entries or clues, and kudos for those who have displayed ingenuity in creating the puzzles.

Incidentally, this game is ideal for two players. Also, the rule for alternating consonants and vowels need not be followed.

COMPETITIVE CROSSWORDS

This is an ideal game for two players, but it can be played by three or more.

In this case, a published crossword puzzle is selected from a recent newspaper or puzzle book. Of course, it should be a crossword that no player has seen before.

Unlike the previous game, the definitions are important in Competitive Crosswords. Let's return to the Smiths. The wife gets the first chance. She peruses the clues and diagram shown opposite.

Mrs. Smith's eyes light upon the definition for 19 Across and she writes in the word FIRECRACKER.

At this point, Mr. Smith has the right to challenge the entry. If his challenge is eventually upheld at the end of the game, he receives 10 points. If his challenge is not upheld, Mrs. Smith scores an extra 10 points.

Mr. Smith does not challenge, hence, his wife scores 11 points—one for each letter in FIRECRACKER.

Now the husband spots the clue "Arcane" at 9 Down. The *C* from FIRECRACKER helps him. He writes in SECRET and gets 6 points for the word plus an extra 5 for crossing FIRECRACKER. The couple is now tied at 11 points apiece.

Mrs. Smith now has a choice. She can decide to cross a smaller word with either SECRET or FIRECRACKER or she can seek a long word elsewhere in the diagram.

The rules and scoring for Competitive Crosswords are as follows:

1. Players take turns filling in words.
2. Players get 1 point for each correct letter filled in and 5 extra points for crossing another word.
3. When an entry is challenged, the decision regarding the validity of the challenge must wait until the end of the game, when the published solution to the puzzle is consulted. If the challenge is upheld, the challenger earns 10 points. If the challenger proves to be wrong, the challenged player receives an extra 10 points.
4. Play continues until the puzzle is completed or until all players are stumped.

The solution to the puzzle used as an example appears on page 212.

ACROSS

1 Exhibit
5 Noisy explosives
10 Declines
14 Aphid, in a way
15 Zola
16 Merge
18 More efficient
19 July 4th noisemaker
21 Electrical unit
22 State, in Strasbourg
24 Seed's appendage
25 Guido's note
26 Dull
28 Model Carol
29 Asian holiday
30 Three, in prescriptions
31 Inchoherent one
34 Rip
36 Moors' kettledrum
38 Flounder
40 Shot at slyly
44 Akin
46 Crown
48 Soap plant
49 Equal: Comb. form
50 Trumpet blast
53 — Abner
54 Burners' locale
57 — de mer
58 Like a satellite's path
61 Dissertations
63 Coagulate
65 Embrace
66 Eft
68 Advanced-study group
70 Mother lode
73 Extension
75 John, to a Scot
76 Custard ingredients
79 Black cuckoo
80 Greek portico
81 Sound of relief
83 Ingest
84 Harsh-sounding
87 Choice
89 Domingo's love
90 Five-of-trumps' game
91 Item of value
92 Weight allowance
93 "Skittle Players" painter
94 Situates

DOWN

1 Serious
2 Hubbubs
3 Carbohydrate's ending
4 " — In the Money"
5 Happen
6 Left out
7 Commune in czarist Russia
8 Ovine utterance
9 Arcane
10 Twofold
11 Corp. letters
12 Stingy one
13 Stone marker
14 Pork fat
17 Cycles
20 Ceremonies
23 Notebook
27 Rum cake
30 Prune
32 Flying mammal
33 Infant's noisy toys
35 Collection
36 Spring up
37 Trials
39 Stole
41 Noisy ghost
42 Inventor Howe
43 Valleys
45 Beaver's handiwork
47 NFL player
51 Berate
52 Spanning
55 Weather follower
56 Cyclone center
59 Prohibition
60 Dies —
62 Long strip
64 Free time
67 NCO's charges
69 House, to Henri
70 Eygptian cotton
71 Not suitable
72 More pleasing
74 "Olympia" painter
77 General Horatio — :
   1727–1806
78 Printer's term
80 Young oyster
82 Stack
85 Metallurgist's concern
86 Stately poem
88 "Fighting Tigers" col.

FILL-INS

This variation of crossword puzzles has many different names and variations. Here is an example of one that I created several decades ago for the Children's Book Council.

Here are the names of some well-known books and authors. Just transfer the underlined words to the right places in the diagram. (You will note that the underlined words are grouped according to size, the two-letter words coming first.) To help you, we have filled in "The Sea Wolf." Start from there.

"Ah Wilderness"
"As You Like It"
"The Mystery at the Black Cat"
"Cyrano de Bergerac"
"Call It Courage"

"Abe Lincoln in Illinois"

"Elephant Bill"
"Jane Eyre"
"Men Like Gods"
Shaw wrote "Saint Joan"
"Here I Stay"

"Twenty Years After"
"The Caine Mutiny"
"Drums"
Dumas wrote "The Three Musketeers"
"At Home In India"
"A Man for Marcy"
O'Hara wrote "My Friend Flicka"
Pease wrote "Secret Cargo"
"Sabre Pilot"
"Big Tiger and Christian"

Austen wrote "Pride and Prejudice"
Barrie wrote "Dear Brutus"
"Big Red"
"The Bridge of San Luis Rey"
Forbes wrote "Johnny Tremain"
Lowell was a famous poet
"The Adventures of Tom Sawyer"
"The Spirit of St. Louis"
"Old Yeller"

Garland wrote "A Son of the Middle Border"
"Microbe Hunters"

"The Last Days of Pompeii"
"On Safari"

"The Big Sky"

"The Alhambra"

The solution appears on page 212.
Several important aspects of this puzzle deserve attention:

1. The black squares are not symmetrical; they are helter-skelter.
2. Unlike American crosswords, some letters are "blind"—in other words, they appear Across but not Down, or vice versa.
3. Such puzzles always have a theme.
4. Usually, these puzzles do not contain numbers in the diagram.

Additionally, it should be pointed out that Fill-Ins are often published without black squares and need not form a perfect square or rectangle.

At this point, please permit me a brief personal digression. When I was giving courses in Language Arts Methods to elementary school teachers at Hunter College and C.C.N.Y., I encouraged them to use Fill-Ins as a way of motivating their pupils.

One of my students was teaching a unit on American Indians. Her homework assignment was to create a Fill-In on the subject. She submitted the following original puzzle.

						S	H	O	S	H	O	N	I
						I				T			
		H	U	R	O	N				O			
						U			C	R	E	E	
				F	O	X			R			R	
					M				E			I	
Y	U	M	A		A		I		E			E	
	O			C	H	E	R	O	K	E	E		
	H				A		O						
A	P	A	C	H	E		Q			T			
L	W	O			M		U			R			
G	K		P		I		O	N	E	I	D	A	
O		P	I	M	A		I			B			
N					M		S	E	N	E	C	A	
Q		L	E	N	I						R		
U	T	E									O		
I							O	T	T	A	W	A	
N	A	V	A	H	O								

I gave the student an A for several reasons. She had included a rather large number of tribes and had crossed them excellently. Also, she had avoided confusion by not trying to crowd the entries into a smaller space.

The student introduced the puzzle in her classroom, using the following procedure: She made a blank diagram on a separate piece of paper and, to give her pupils a start, she wrote in IROQUOIS. Below the diagram, she listed all the entries in alphabetical order. She duplicated enough copies for all her pupils and asked them to fill in the words.

Later the student told me that some of her brighter pupils made up their own Fill-Ins!

BRASS MONKEY

Brass Monkey is a different kind of word game because it requires a good memory more than a good vocabulary. It is an excellent party game—in fact, the more the merrier. Also, one of its advantages is that it doesn't require paper and pencils.

The object of the game is to be the only person not eliminated. To start Brass Monkey, the group should agree on some large category, such as plants, birds, fish, writers, movie stars, athletes, clothing, etc. Players draw lots to decide the order in which they play. A good idea is to have a deck of cards handy. The player who draws the highest card goes first.

Now let us say that a group of five players has chosen "animals" as a category. Their task is to name animals in alphabetical order.

Linda starts the game. She calls *aardvark*. Ralph is next. He must repeat *aardvark* and call an animal beginning with *b*. He says, *"Aardvark, bear."* Get the idea? Here's how it goes:

> Linda: Aardvark
> Ralph: Aardvark, bear
> Tony: Aardvark, bear, cougar
> Norma: Aardvark, bear, cougar, dog

Paul, who is next, cannot think of an animal beginning with *e*. He is eliminated and becomes a *brass monkey*.

Now it's Linda's turn again. She skips the *e* and calls an animal beginning with *f*.

> Linda: Aardvark, bear, cougar, dog, brass monkey, fox
> Ralph: Aardvark, bear, cow. . . .

At that point, Ralph is eliminated because he forgot that cougar was the correct call. Now it's Tony's turn. Since Ralph's letter was *g* Tony must call an animal beginning with *h*.

> Tony: Aardvark, bear, cougar, dog, brass monkey, fox, brass monkey, hyena

As the game proceeds, it becomes harder and harder for the players to remember the sequence or the names of the animals and the position of the brass monkeys. Sooner or later only one person is left. He or she is the winner.

SCAVENGER HUNT

You may wonder what connection this game has with words. Well, it really depends on the persons who organize the hunt.

Once again, perhaps it is best to cite a personal experience as an example. Many years ago when our daughter Merryl was in high school, she invited nine of her classmates to spend a weekend at our summer home near Cape Cod. Before the group arrived, my wife and I prepared a scavenger hunt for two teams of five each.

The teams were called Red and Blue. Each group elected a captain as they assembled in the living room. The captain of the Red team was given a red card marked #1, and the other captain was given a #1 blue card. They were told that each card contained a clue that would lead them to some spot on our property where another card would await them with a second clue.

My wife and I had previously placed red and blue cards inside and outside the house. Incidentally, one of the rules was that if a team accidentally came upon the other team's card, they were forbidden to disturb it or even read it.

Clue #1 for the Red team read:

> Go to a spot beginning with *B*
> Where Nature has left its own debris.
> Look underneath for a cardboard clue
> That will lead you to Clue Number 2.

The first card for the Blue team contained a simple cryptogram with the code explained. It read: "B = A, C = B, D = C, etc. Here's the message. M P P L V O E F S U I F Q P S D I."

Clue #2 for the Red team consisted of a riddle. It read:

> I was an acorn once upon a time,
> Go in the back and make a short climb.

For the Blue team's second clue, another riddle read:

> "I often follow salt, but I'm also a rhyme for the opposite of a person who buys things."

My point is that each clue in that Scavenger Hunt became a word game. I should also tell you that the clues for the two teams were placed strategically so that it would be hard for one group to stumble over the other's clue accidentally.

What was the prize? Each teenager received a pocket dictionary.

By the way, if one of the above four clues has stumped you, the answers are on page 212.

CLOSE ENOUGH

This word game, which I invented, has a history. When I was an English teacher in a Harlem junior high school, an assistant principal suddenly appeared at my door and wheeled in about thirty-five abridged dictionaries.

"Mr. Maleska," he said, "I want you to familiarize your classes with the use of the dictionary and I expect to see the methods you will use in your lesson plans."

The all-boys class in front of me groaned. Dictionaries! To them, such tomes seemed like the dullest books on earth.

That night I tossed in my sleep. How could I make lexicons lively enough to create interest in them? Then an idea occurred to me. As a start, I would play "Stick the Teacher" with the boys!

The next day I distributed the dictionaries and explained the game that we were about to play. On the blackboard I wrote:

TEACHER   CLASS

The boys were then asked to look through the books and try to find a word that I wouldn't know. If they succeeded, a point would be recorded under CLASS. If not, I would get a point.

The brightest members of the class immediately turned to the *X* section. One of them called out *xebec*. Luckily my crossword-puzzle experience came to my aid. I described it as "a Mediterranean sailing vessel." The questioner shook his head in disgust. I marked 1 point under TEACHER.

The next boy stumped me. He gave me *xanthic* and I mixed it up with *xyloid*. "Woody," I answered.

"Man, you lose," he replied. "It says here that it means yellow or yellowish."

I recorded 1 point under CLASS. The battle went on for the entire period. As I recall the score was tied when the bell rang. I had learned the meaning of several words previously unfamiliar to me and the boys had discovered that a dictionary could actually be fun.

From that experience, Close Enough evolved as a party game I have played several times with fellow word lovers. The rules are simple.

1. One player becomes the arbiter. He decides whether the answer given is "close enough" to the definition in the dictionary, which he consults.
2. An *abridged* dictionary must be used. Also, all foreign or obsolete words

should be excluded, as well as those that only a top scientist would know.

3. Teams take turns looking into the dictionary to choose a word that their rivals may not know.

4. Points are scored as in the above Teacher vs. Class example.

Here are some examples from a recent party:

Team 1: Syzygy.
Team 2: It has something to do with astronomy.
Arbiter: Correct, but too vague. One-half point.

The correct answer was: "the conjunction or opposition of two heavenly bodies; any pair of opposites."

Team 2: Sylvatic.
Team 1: Pertaining to a forest.
Arbiter: Close enough. The true definition is, "Of or in the woods or affecting the animals there. One point."

Obviously, the arbiter's role in this game is crucial. His or her decisions can lead to debates. If someone like Billy Martin were in my living room, he might be tempted to kick dust on the arbiter!

WHAT IF YOU WERE ... ?

Before this game starts, the host should prepare a list of subjects (see list under Categories on page 23). Some examples are flowers, insects, animals, trees, birds, or pieces of machinery. While the group agrees on a subject, the host gives a 5″ × 7″ card and a pencil to each guest.

Let us say that "birds" has been chosen by the group. Each player now writes:

"If I were a bird, I'd like to be a . . ."

Players continue the sentence with their own choices of birds and then write why they have made such choices.

After all players have finished writing, the host collects the cards, shuffles them and reads them one by one.

Players now vote on the most interesting statement or, in some cases, the most humorous one. This game, by the way, often reveals the hidden desires of individuals and other aspects of their psyches.

WHO AM I?

Years ago, one of the most enjoyable and hilarious nights I've ever spent occurred when the host at a party introduced Who Am I? to a group of about eight people.

He had previously prepared cards, each of which contained the name of a famous person, living or dead. He shuffled the cards, gave one to each of us, and warned us not to let anyone else see our mystery celebrities.

Then he told us that the game was a combination of Charades and Twenty Questions. Players must take turns giving oblique oral hints concerning the names of the persons on their cards and/or acting out certain special aspects or traits of their celebrities. Meanwhile, the others were allowed to ask pertinent questions, but not permitted to name a specific person until they were absolutely sure.

As it happened, an obese male in the group had drawn Marilyn Monroe. He swiveled his hips around the room and made gestures indicating that his chest had enlarged. We soon guessed *his* celebrity!

Another guest started out by saying "Well!" That was before Ronald Reagan had become a politician, so we were reasonably sure that the mystery celebrity was a certain comedian. Then the guest pretended to be playing a violin. One of us finally asked, "Do you know Rochester?" When that question received a nod, we knew that the celebrity was Jack Benny.

Actually, unlike most other games, there were not many rules. Our host wisely let us go with the flow. Try it sometime. It should be fun!

Solo Games and Games for Two

Just as some of the Party Games can be played by only one or two people, it is also true that many of the games listed in this chapter can be played by several people at the same time. It is my hope that readers will be tolerant enough to recognize the difficulty in trying to separate games into different categories.

WORDS WITHIN A WORD

As the opener in this section, I wish I could have thought of a more scintillating name for the game. At any rate, it's a pastime that has entranced me for many decades.

The object of the game is to create as many small words as possible from a long word. Take VOCABULARY, for example. How many words can you find that use the letters in that word? Note that the *A* appears twice. Thus, LAVA is acceptable. I've given it a whirl and have come up with sixty-seven little words that can be built within the framework of the large word. I can imagine that several readers will exceed my total, but I had lots of pleasure finding those sixty-seven words. By the way, the minimum is a *four-letter* word. Obsolete words, foreign words and proper names are excluded. For example CALVARY would not be accepted, nor would CUBA or URAL or YALU.

My sources are *Webster's New International Dictionary, Second Edition* and *Webster's Third New International Dictionary*. A list of my sixty-seven words appears on page 212.

If you would like to score yourself, here are my estimations:

30 words   Fair
40 words   Good
50 words   Very good
60 words   Excellent
70 words   Super-duper!

ANIMALS IN HIDING

Here's a word game with a tricky twist that I have invented: Under SOLUTION write the answer for each definition. Then find the hidden beast and place it under ANIMAL

DEFINITION	SOLUTION	ANIMAL
1. Prepare an ambush	— — — — — — — — —	— — — —
2. Disaster	— — — — — — — — — — — —	— — —
3. Northeast U.S.	— — — — — — — — —	— — —
4. Sea off Alaska	— — — — — —	— — — —
5. Have a crush on	— — — — — —	— — — — — —
6. Raucous, grating	— — — — — —	— — — — — —
7. Rigid; stern	— — — — — — —	— — — — — —
8. Gangster's ''exit''	— — —	— — — —
9. Do some plastering	— — — —	— — — —
10. Scram	— — — — — —	— — — — —

Warning: Some of the answers involve puns, part-words or homophones. Here are a few examples:

DEFINITION	SOLUTION	ANIMAL
City official	mayor	mare
Man of La Mancha	Don Quixote	donkey
Long-run musical	hair	hare
Louisiana creek	bayou	ewe
Like a fanatic	rabid	rabbit

The answers appear on page 213. Score yourself as follows:

6 Fair
7 Good
8 Very good
9 Excellent
10 Perfect!

SAID THE BIRD

Said the Bird was contributed by Ms. Barbara A. Vought, a puzzle fan who lives in a sylvan spot in upstate New York and has spent many years watching our feathered friends.

See if you can identify these North American birds by their statements.

If you knew my name you'd think I . . .

1. am a church official _____

2. keep the baby warm _____

3. go well with rolls _____

4. am a flag for sailing _____

5. am a slow-witted grape masher _____

6. am a German official _____

7. talk to a girl in a yellow bikini _____

8. drop Mrs. Rogers _____

9. am a loud-mouthed hoist _____

10. cut a senior citizen's hair _____

11. am a disturbed girl singer _____

12. am the rear of a tent _____

13. sneak through beehives _____

14. am an athlete with a bad sunburn _____

15. try to emulate a hunter _____

16. am a flying apparatus with a light end _____

17. hate to see a cat sleep _____

18. am an armed marine vessel _____

19. am a chicken on a rainy day _____

20. sit on acorns _____

21. would interest an ancient Indian _____

22. play baseball _____

23. prefer riding to flying   _____

24. am scared   _____

25. am part of a fence down South   _____

26. remind you of Arthur Godfrey   _____

27. play hockey for Detroit   _____

28. play a flute on the beach alone   _____

29. would be good on a road crew   _____

30. sound like a priest's hat   _____

31. sound like a young visitor from outer space   _____

32. am a mud wrestler   _____

33. beat my child   _____

34. look like a jaundiced giraffe   _____

35. am a muscular action of the throat   _____

Score yourself as follows:

25 or more   Remarkable
20–24   Excellent
15–19   Good
10–14   Fair
Below 10   For the birds!

The answers appear on page 213.

MISTER 5 × 5

Mel Thorner, an attorney who specialized in diagramless puzzles, sent me an interesting original creation just before he passed away.

Mister 5 × 5 is rather easy, but I had fun solving it as a change of pace from brain-boggling puzzles. Even though there are only a few crossings, you should be able to solve all or most of the twenty words in the puzzle. The average score is 15.

The solution appears on page 213.

ACROSS

1 Flash
3 Slider, for example
5 Beef quality
6 Senior
8 Washed
10 Lovers' meeting
12 Mohammedan bible
14 Tissue swelling
15 Sea duck
16 Very bad

DOWN

1 Rubbed-in dirt
2 Small candle
3 Fishing basket
4 Improve by editing
7 Seven times a week
9 Bravery
10 Once and once again
11 Belonging to others
12 Down-under marsupial
13 Dynamite inventor

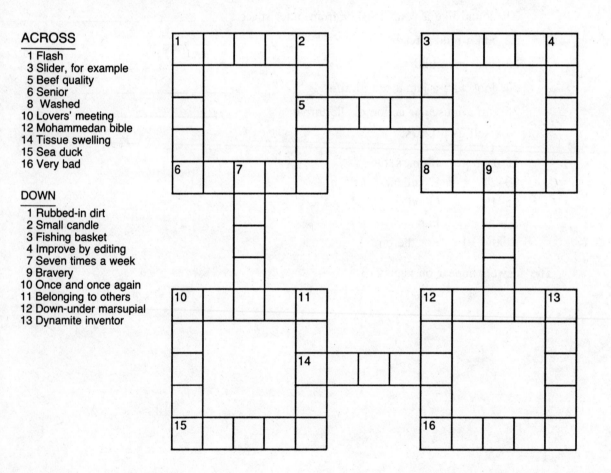

CRYPTOGRAMS

Ever since I was a teenager, I have been entranced by coded messages—and during my lifetime I have courted two wives by sending them cryptograms.

My first wife, Jean, was a Latin major in college and a genuine wordsmith. We met as freshmen at Montclair State Teachers College, and I fell in love with her at first sight. After discovering her penchant for words, I sent her one or two personal crossword puzzles (my very first attempts) and dozens of cryptograms. Sometimes I would slip one to her in the middle of a boring biology class.

When Jean died, I met Annrea—a fine portrait artist and the daughter of John Rea Neill, the illustrator of most of the *Oz* books. Annrea was not a wordsmith, and so I had to teach her how to solve cryptograms. In her case, I always preceded the message with a coded "Dearest Annrea," or "Beloved Annrea," in order to give her a start.

I have also made a small amount of money on this type of puzzle. In the thirties and forties, the *Herald Tribune* paid me one dollar for each coded message that was accepted. The cryptograms were always printed underneath the crossword puzzle. I guess my efforts were published at least fifteen times.

At any rate, let me tell you that it's not easy to create really good cryptograms. In the first place, to be fair to the solver, every letter should be repeated at least once. However, sometimes that rule is disregarded if only one or two letters are "unkeyed" and can be easily guessed by the context.

Secondly, the coded message should be interesting or informative or even inspirational. The worst letdown for a solver is to unravel a statement that is blah!

As the editor of puzzles for *The New York Times,* I have received hundreds of requests from devotees of cryptograms asking me to include them. The problem is that there is no room on the puzzle page in the Sunday magazine for an additional brainteaser. Also, the appearance of a cryptogram in the daily newspaper would cause the elimination of a profit-making advertisement.

All the above has led me to include in this section a veritable feast for lovers of codes. Below you will find numerous cryptograms that I have created just for this book.

At this point, let me give a few tips to the readers who have never tackled this sort of puzzle.

1. If a one-letter word appears, it is usually an A or an I. Try A first. If it leads to trouble, switch to I.
2. Watch for ING endings.
3. If a letter appears only once or twice and is always at the end of a word, try a Y.
4. If a three-letter word is repeated, try THE.
5. If a three-letter word comes between two long words, take a chance on AND.
6. Study the message carefully. If you see that a certain letter appears very often and is seldom or never at the beginning of a word, but crops up at the ends of words or in the middle, it's probably an E.
7. Compare two-letter words. If you think that K should become E at the end of one word, but another two-letter word begins with K, switch to O. Incidentally, TO is often used.
8. Look for double letters and repeating letters. A good example is O G M-M O B. The best bet is LITTLE!
9. If a three-letter word seems to end in U, try YOU.
10. Apostrophes are your friends. The letter after the apostrophe is either an S or a T. If it's a four-letter word, bet on the T and try either CAN'T or DON'T or maybe WON'T. If it's a long word, S is most likely.
11. Watch for words beginning with TH. If the code has X P C X, for instance, try THAT. If it's X M P L P, a good guess would be THERE.
12. If you spot a four-letter word that has a first letter which is repeated only once in the puzzle, it's apt to be either WITH or FROM. The same is true with regard to a three-letter word. Your best guess would be FOR.
13. S is a letter that often starts or ends words. When you spot a coded letter that fits the start-finish category, try the S.
14. When long words occur, look for suffixes like TION and MENT or LY. As for LY, REALLY is often repeated in the messages. On seeing Z B J O O V, for example, you should take a stab at REALLY.
15. If a letter appears only at the beginning of a word, try a J.
16. Do not get discouraged if your first attempts prove fruitless. Study the answer and see where you went wrong. As the saying goes, practice makes perfect.

There are many other tips that I could give to new solvers, but let me quote the philosopher-educator John Dewey. He said, "We learn by doing." If you have never solved cryptograms, you are missing lots of enjoyment. When the solution starts to unravel, you feel the thrill of accomplishment. Unlike crossword puzzles, it's usually an all-or-nothing situation. That kind of complete triumph puts you on top of the world!

Here are 50 cryptograms that I have created for you. As far as possible, they are graded from *easy* to *hard*. The answers are listed on page 213–14.

1. QW QC AQWWQRB WKJW AQDCW-BDJPG WGJXKGDC CKNSMP ZG

    JZMG QRCWDSXWNDC.

2. WKG PZVC XGB WH ZYY AHB VT: PZXG PZCB HWKGJT WJFYB

    AHBHFT.

3. QTA YBA ZAWZKA JC XWOYWC ZTWCA YW OZJKK YBA XAQCO?

4. YPU'R RJWB EPPYBU UVXWBNG. EAO? ZBXJCGB OPC EPCNY

    MFPZJZNO QBR GMNVURBFG JNPUQ RAB EJO.

5. MC QRCFJ Q LXZXBMKG HQFBMXJ CJCL, HPM Q KFMMKX

    RQBFKKQ FB GCPL HQFBM ZQB.

6. WBPK PBAZKY BGEKF WQAK SWBIKYBPK JWQHPY GBH

    GQPZIZKY SWB SZYW EB HKPZFZYJK.

7. HLFKQE KY LFLP AMTQMU ZPELYLTE ZP TCKYET KGELP

    CYKFZHLT LTAMCL GYKJ EYKQNULTKJL CYKNULJT.

8. GRUZZY AJLVRLAKY AJKLGQG SZAVZSRU SQKRUQJ: GUQ UKG

    RYKGG!

9. FP LQWR PBB GDYKZQVQDF BGCZV BWPC TXHQWV PW

    TXHQWZFFZV, YGF VPCZ NXDZHQW XD Q SXH SPLK PW

    VXCXKQW NZVVZK.

10. OSHTUJ LKTJQY OHPSJQYL, DGLQTUJ VR DTUOPDL YPOGR
    GKDGRL JMUMHGYML HGTU YPVPHHPD.

11. HMZQK, BUU-MZRGZQZX UVKXUJQX QZGQBRVKXH BXUZ
    QJJRZQH.

12. AJMOZS UTQLJHMJNLZ UBKQQLJU CMZAB OKJ UCKGGLV AMVU
    KJ GPYU: QKPUKV HMS GTJN PVUPYL.

13. CXKT CLFJG QJSGZWLSM UGBJGFG SJHJQ ZGKMLSM ZLPBQ
    GFGKWPXBBT SGFJFG ''UJH-UXKKGQ GSX.''

14. SZJ AJZGCLRM HKJZ UJQB LJRPU WP MJHXM AJRPU QJS
    ZJPUGCLRM PGZ ''MGXBKGB'' JP MWLG.

15. QV ZHAHBQVQSU HBQA SJ USZ? Q TKJH, MHZ JHKAAM TKUUSZ
    ZHAA.

16. OBZUM PVCJSZUH ZIQJPD: MT CDZQD WTM YTTI TVM YTU BTUD
    MWZS MGT WTVUO JO STM QDUH GJOD, GD ZUD MTCI.

17. QZVJ BGBQPR FGN KPJZWQ, FGN WKRQLZWWF VZNMQ ZP
    NPHGQRKV ''KPMHKLZRKGP.''

18. AZUKS FLILUINQL PLZFNGB HSGQLF ABHILPB SW ILGLQNHNSW.
    HS JKZI LGHL NH WLJ?

19. HF GZZ BVGKLGTLB, CM UNQGKB BUXNZL GZCGFB HM UNQGKM:
    XVUMTCJBM CUF GTM CM UMTM XK MGTVU?

20. UJZBQB PH MKUM-USPJHL UGWZIP UGWZL PH UPSUZPJB
    BKUMQ KH IZGJQKYJC YCPXZS UGSLZH LPXH IZCPX.

21. ZQHJ UTTEH ZTF'C CWNZ AJJI TG UWQUEJF TF EQCUWJF
    UTKFCJGH AJUNKHJ TI ANUCJGQN.

22. QA OJGLOJSS GRJRQGRQMG, RZULL-OJGL MSBKRG JUL PKMZ
    UJULU RZJA ZBPL-UKA OSJGRG.

23. AQUPBY VJGKQ APMZUV RKVZUMZ CLUZZ MPJPRGV TPSSZU VL-
    QUTV QC JSRVZ UQBYZ.

24. KBPG VUWPK VWKQZB SGVQRGK PQHJM SGLTQSG CWVBZ
    KUWCK WMBR SWMJGS UWSHG LTWJBHK.

25. FGAJJY, TJVHK ZRYHDVTQRHY JB LQDC YTGPP YZAQ, XJ
    MDJLZXQ, BVR BJD KGMMC PZHHPQ HCFQY.

26. ZBJACUL TJL JATPMU JADJLM NH HZBJUHQ DCUG DPKUG CR
    QPAAJKM, NBU RPU ZBJRUCUL.

27. AGBU SBWJH YGBUK ZEQPWEQ AGU IGEJAWKY SBJPP KJZK GA
    IWQ HUGBIPJK.

28. CUXZOVGCM COSZU BZPFZMWVOL, XYDSHUVQ FHKT
    CUGYOVLVVU KOZGGHX BZDL, TZJV YGKVU JVNVQ DZUP KZNH
    QOHJVOL.

29. ZMLHQ DML CLLR XBJ QXZ KB MLWWSDLLJ MLRQH RXS
    QXHKWS UQ ZQCRQJ "HZXC ULXCJQCH."

30. AJQSYO HPLVZQP MV JZQ LHZA LMZTPT OQPMV
    "PMQSVMVSJY."

My favorite cryptograms are those in which one or two of the coded letters may contain a hint concerning the message. For example, in #31, D O Z Y O N E suggests that the subject is sleep, and in #32 the word C R A S H arouses curiosity as to whether some kind of accident is the topic. All the cryptograms that follow have either a direct or indirect clue in at least one coded word.

31. XPCZE QJZ-NXZE NCPLZ ND YPPY NYE DOZY ONE N QJDDQZ
LJZLDN.

32. BCUD CJX RCUD RUASKOH CRASH JASKOH RSH DHCUD CJX
DBCUD.

33. MEETBOOBS ABLURBT UGLYKBS: "ARB MIGH XLH AM ORZA
ARBK ZE YO AM ORMZA ARBK SMXI!"

34. PM AGRR UMMFH BAAYED UMMPH MA AXDAGR EBFXFYH?

35. WAGONS-GO EARCAS WRYCCNS GO EYOWRNCW.

36. IZBTZ TKNOH-ZUBNAY INAGROAN UR XNUPY TUPHSP HAOOAY:
"XSNXASKG XASNXA!"?

37. BY ARMY, BOOKRMMENT AKETOM NUUKRMMENT BTC
CRUKRMMENT.

38. STEED EQUAL ITPUNS, NSQ IZD PYLUXZPPD EQXYIQ AZLLD.

39. BUMRAP NUSPGTSUER SNUTTE: OTTE MBATO GUTTER ETNUTT
MB NUTTE.

40. HEGRR REDWAY SAUCE XDUDPUP EGPY FW XEDPPFWH RCE
XFWWDE PADWD.

41. ARRI AWINE GWESRO SN AIMED STIRR IMEDU SN TMU
GROOMED.

42. ILLBULLED LUSDY ADO LIBDO EDDA ULLEDY LO BVD LBVDY
DOS.

43. NITWIT USESWIG: PHENO XIUB XSBHSNNO WIT PIPPO BIG.

44. HIDE BERDONTEETEWY SKKU STUD YNSTEADOY, HKBSR-CD
    YNOTEADOY YIKBSR CD WKKR.

45. TART TARTY BKOOSH RB OKH TASTY NKI TARNISH: "TASKI!"

46. SWOECAS ANNICYH AWKS UECYI PAINU HOCUN KWE "KWENCHY
    PUN."

47. IKKY ZANY KO HKKE HAZYKUTS BUBITZ YSNU ZBETZUBO.

48. ANTIBOY ACTI IKKY OBYASKI INDID TBZ STANSNZ DUKID TD
    "UKU'D TCI."

49. GNYK ANY OU-GUY MY A-TOMCAT TAMC GK GCT.

50. CPAARAT OXPAT CPAS TIRUO NXUM IMPUN: "R SRM: OXP
    AXN."

CRYPTOCROSSWORDS

Many solvers of crossword puzzles like to have a quotation built into the diagram. Others enjoy cryptograms, as well. To meet the desires of the various groups, I have invented Cryptocrosswords. This new type of puzzle has been published in *The New York Times* and in Dell puzzle magazines.

Opposite is a Cryptocrossword for you to solve.

Directions: Using the Down clues, fill in as many words as possible in the blank diagram. Try to begin with a word that you are reasonably sure of. (Note that no Across clues are given.)

After getting a start, consult the coded diagram on the left and compare the letters with the ones you have filled in. Thus, if you have placed a *T* in the first box for 1 Down, the coded letter in that spot stands for *T*.

Your next step is to convert into *T* in the blank diagram all the coded letters that are identical with the one at 1 Down. This should lead to new insights. Gradually, the complete solution will emerge.

After solving the puzzle, you will find part of a quotation from Richard Brinsley Sheridan at 11, 40 and 28 Across.

The solution appears on page 214.

DOWN

1 Rio ——, city in Brazil
2 Eskimo boat
3 Type of firearm
4 Compass point
5 Gudrun's sovereign
6 Rum cocktail: 2 wds.
7 Tolkien creature
8 George Meredith heroine
9 Famed first name in Ireland
10 Rival of Foyt, Unser, et al.
17 Film directed by George
    Stevens: 1952
20 Homestead, for one
22 Kaydets' home: abbr.
24 U.S. naval officer who
    invented a gyroscopic
    steering-gear for torpedoes
25 Space capsule's interior
26 Battle-scarred Ethiopian town
27 College in Weston, Mass.
29 Encrusts
30 Smart follower
31 Pineapples, mints or maids
34 Slack part of a sail
37 Town in Nigeria
39 Biblical captain

1 Z	2 B	3 A	4 X	5 Y	■	6 O	7 M	8 I	9 G	10 X
11 Q	O	B	X	Z	■	12 Y	C	Q	Y	E
13 E	Q	H	G	A	■	14 Q	J	Y	O	G
15 Z	Y	G	■	16 Q	17 X	Z	■	18 E	M	K
19 M	L	C	20 Y	■	21 N	Y	22 K	Y	E	Y
■	■	■	23 J	24 N	Y	Q	O	■	■	■
25 J	26 Y	27 C	Z	M	E	■	28 Q	29 J	30 Y	31 E
32 Y	I	G	■	33 U	34 G	X	■	35 Y	A	Y
36 S	M	H	37 Q	G	■	38 A	39 Q	L	G	E
40 Q	U	Q	A	A	■	41 Y	C	G	J	Y
42 E	Y	X	Y	A	■	43 S	Y	X	L	X

1	2	3	4	5	■	6	7	8	9	10
11					■	12				
13					■	14				
15			■	16	17		■	18		
19			20	■	21		22			
■	■	■	23	24				■	■	■
25	26	27				■	28	29	30	31
32			■	33	34		■	35		
36			37		■	38	39			
40					■	41				
42					■	43				

CRYPTOMATHS

Here's another of my inventions. Each Cryptomath is based on a mathematical progression or formula that may increase, decrease or go both ways. Simple examples are: 2-4-6-8 or 8-6-4-2 or 2-4-6-8-6-4-2.

The object is to find the hidden person, place or thing by figuring out the formula. In the following Cryptomath, the last name of a famous author is concealed among the names of six other writers.

Keep in mind that the order of the six names is important.

```
C  O  L  E  R  I  D  G  E
H  A  R  D  Y
K  E  A  T  S
H  A  W  T  H  O  R  N  E
S  T  E  I  N  B  E  C  K
F  A  U  L  K  N  E  R
```

In this next case, the object is to find the name of a well-known literary hero concealed among seven other names from literature. Again, the order of the names is important.

```
I  S  O  L  D  E
S  I  L  V  E  R
N  E  R  I  S  S  A
H  A  R  R  I  N  G  T  O  N
A  S  T  R  O  P  H  E  L
A  T  H  O  S
E  A  R  W  I  C  K  E  R
```

The answers to both Cryptomaths appear on page 214.

SCANAGRAMS

Here's another one of my inventions. In each of the couplets below, one of the words is an anagram for the word to be filled in. To give you a start, the word to be unscrambled in the first couplet is *canoe*. The answers appear on page 214.

1. *Caution, Hiawatha!*
   Your frail canoe may quickly tip
   If you should take that _____ trip!

2. *Until the Fur Flies*
   A girl who wears a _____ may
   Attempt to look a bit blasé.

3. *Beware the Ides*
   March has a certain _____ about it,
   Though Caesar's ghost will surely doubt it.

4. *Where Is the Rascal Cook?*
   Said Papa, and his voice was gruff,
   "This steak _____ not to be so tough!"

5. *The Whole Truth*
   The timid witness did not curse,
   And yet he _____ . Now, was that worse?

6. *Olympics*
   For athletes strong and simon-pure,
   The _____ wreath has great allure.

7. *How to Succeed . . .*
   If you should aspire to jobs that are higher,
   Then _____ the boss though you may be a liar.

8. *Under the Christmas Tree*
   Now listen, you can almost hear
   The _____ tinkling in your ear.

9. *School Daze*
   The dullard, _____ and the pest
   Can make a teacher need a rest.

10. *B. C. Burner*
    'Tis _____ that Mauna Loa
    Erupted once in the time of Noah.

LITERARY SCANAGRAMS

Bibliophiles may enjoy this offshoot of ordinary Scanagrams. The directions are the same but the subjects of the couplets are authors, books, characters, etc. The answers appear on page 214.

1. *Sail On!*
   In _____ milieux O'Neill could not remain;
   Far greater things were blazing in his brain.

2. *After the Ball*
   While Scott and Zelda _____ about,
   The lights of joy were burning out.

3. *Long Years' Journey*
   "Bad _____ !" the prudish judges state,
   But Joyce's *Ulysses* continues to rate.

4. *Sic Transit . . .*
   The _____ books are no longer hip,
   But once he had large readership.

5. *No Doubt of It, Thomas!*
   In your first novel, the reader gleans
   The _____ views of home in many scenes.

6. *Oliver's Twist*
   The _____ rode in something crude;
   No, 'tisn't true that he canoed!

7. *What the Dickens!*
   His _____ reveals he knew the ropes;
   His plots could fit the TV soaps.

8. *The Fop Who Flopped*
   Malvolio, with the best of _____ ,
   Goes strutting in cross-gartered hose.

9. *The Odd Couple*
   _____ and Juliet form one of the pairs
   In Shakespeare's troths and love affairs.

10. *A Safe Bet*
    Alcott's chillun had lots of charm;
    The little _____ girls meant nobody harm.

11. *The King and the Sting*
_____ should have known whose love was real,
And who was out to wheel and deal.

12. *Dracula*
Bram Stoker's hero scares the reader;
The man's _____ may cause a bleeder.

13. *"The Cenci"*
Though _____ isn't the nicest theme,
The Shelley drama made critics beam.

14. *Versatile Parisian*
Some rank Sartre as the _____ writer:
Philosopher, teacher and underground fighter.

15. *"Androcles and the Lion"*
Among dramatic _____ of man and beast,
The one by GBS is not the least.

16. *The Green-Eyed Monster*
When nothing _____ Othello's rage,
The beast within bursts out onstage.

17. *In "The Rivals"*
Bob _____ growls and blusters like a bear,
But in the end he's not so hard to scare.

18. *Mystery Writer*
Some marble slabs above the _____ heroes lie;
For example, read *Epitaph for a Spy*.

19. *Another Writer*
Though I start with a King, I'm not from Siam;
My name is _____ ; now guess who I am.

20. *Or Maybe Shaw*
From _____ wars he seldom rested;
Think T. E. Lawrence and you've guessed it.

Just for good measure, here's an easy one with no blank space. Find the anagram that fits the name.

That Wharton Man
His sled ride ended 'neath a tree,
Resulting in ménage for three.

LIT-O-GRAMS

While we're in a literary mood, let's go back to cryptograms. In this kind of puzzle a quotation from a work by a famous author is coded. The author's name appears at the bottom, and the source is underlined beneath his or her name.

Incidentally, it's not easy to find a Lit-O-Gram in which every letter is repeated somewhere. But #1 fulfills all the requirements.

My suggestion is that you start with Q H H and compare it with Q O and Q L A.

1. SDAI JPL LAHQOFRAM QLA QO DJEA, SA DQRA OJ ODFIG JB QHH

    ODAFL CJJZ KJFIOM JL FO SJPHZ XA FEKJMMFXHA OJ AIZPLA

    ODAE. XPO SDAI ODAT QLA QSQT, SA YJIMJHA JPLMAHRAM BJL

    ODAFL QXMAIYA XT ZSAHHFIC JI ODAFL RFYAM.

    —XALIQLZ MDQS

    DAQLOXLAQG DJPMA

The second Lit-O-Gram contains a slight problem. The third letter in V K F V M Y is not repeated elsewhere. However, you can easily guess it from the context.

2. JWYXHQC, XVHX AWBQG PWQQWA JM,

    QWZM ZKYXBM, CVM HQWEM KC PYMM,

    CVM IHE XMHIV LM VWA XW IQKJO

    VKFVMY XVHE XVM CDVMYL IVKJM;

    WY, KP ZKYXBM PMMOQM AMYM,

    VMHZ'E KXCMQP AWBQG CXWWD XW VMY.

    —JKQXWE

    IWJBC

Another piece of poetry is featured in the third *Lit-O-Gram*. To get started you might want to unravel the poet's name by comparing the letters with some of the ones repeated in the two-letter words.

3. BSPQS; QAYS PXPH; EVS DAZU AK XAS

           WD PKESC PGG PZ SPCEVGH DAZU;

           BSPQS; QAYS PXPH; XS RA VWY XCAZU

    EA DWZU DA XWGRGH . . .

    —ESZZHDAZ

    <u>WZ YSYACWPY</u>

The answers to all three Lit-O-Grams appear on page 215.

UNSCRAMBLE-LIT

Continuing on the literary trail, let's try another invention of mine. Listed below are the last names of eleven American writers. Using the *first or last* letters of each, can you find the full name of another American writer? The letters in the writer's name appear in orderly fashion. For example, the first name of the writer must begin with either *R* or *D*

DREISER	WILDER	O'NEILL
O'HARA	TWAIN	DOS PASSOS
BELLOW	FAULKNER	WESTCOTT
UPDIKE	WILBUR	

That one was probably too easy. In this case, eight Shakespearean characters are listed so that the letters you need appear in a *scrambled* order. Using the first and last letters, can you find another of The Bard's characters whose name has eight letters?

HOLOFERNES	NERISSA	MICHAEL
URSULA	OPHELIA	PORTIA
IMOGEN	BASSANIO	

Was the last one too hard? Maybe you'll do better with this nineteenth-century British writer whose last name has nine letters. Once again, the letters in the writer's name are *scrambled* in the list. Here are nine other British writers.

SOUTHEY	SCOTT	KIPLING
AUDEN	SPENSER	BRONTE
ADDISON	MEREDITH	CONGREVE

The answers to the three examples of Unscramble-Lit appear on page 215.

FIRST-LETTER SCRAMBLE

This puzzle is a variation of the preceding one. Now you are asked to concentrate only on the *first letters* in the list. Using those letters from the names of ten American authors, can you unscramble the *full name* of a male character created by another American writer?

ALCOTT	NORRIS
EMERSON	ODETS
GLASGOW	RAWLINGS
IRVING	THURBER
LEWIS	VIDAL

This time the titles of works by Sir Walter Scott are listed. Using the *first letter* of each title, can you unscramble the *full name* of another British author?

MARMION

LEGEND OF MONTROSE (THE)

HEART OF MIDLOTHIAN (THE)

LADY OF THE LAKE (THE)

CASTLE DANGEROUS

BLACK DWARF (THE)

SURGEON'S DAUGHTER (THE)

ANTIQUARY (THE)

EVE OF SAINT JOHN (THE)

REDGAUNTLET

ABBOT (THE)

Listed below are the names of eight Shakespearean characters. Using the *first letter* of each, can you unscramble the name of a famous place in a Shakespearean play?

SCROOP	NERISSA
ENOBARBUS	EDGAR
IAGO	ROSALIND
OTHELLO	LEAR

The answers appear on page 215.

VERTICAL-LIT

The names of twelve famous writers are listed *vertically*. Unscrambling the letters in one of the *horizontal* rows, can you find the *full name* of another great writer?
The answer appears on page 215.

```
H  W  S  S  S  L  T  F  E  D  C  C
A  H  T  A  A  O  R  A  M  R  O  H
G  I  E  N  L  N  O  U  E  E  L  E
G  T  I  T  I  G  L  L  R  I  E  S
A  M  N  A  N  F  L  K  S  S  R  T
R  A  B  Y  G  E  O  N  O  E  I  E
D  N  E  A  E  L  P  E  N  R  D  R
   C  N  R  L  E  R           G  T
   K  A     O                 E  O
   W                          N
```

LITERAQUEST

PHILOSTRATE is the master of the revels in *A Midsummer Night's Dream*. Using the letters in his name, how many other Shakespearean *characters* can you find? The average score is 6; a score of 10 or more is excellent.

Note that the letter *T* is the only one that may be repeated in the name of a character.
The answer appears on page 215.

BRIEF QUIZZES

For a change of pace, here are five questions. The first three are rather well-known.

1. What eight-letter word contains only one vowel?
2. Can you name two words that contain A-E-I-O-U, in that order?
3. What three words end in -gry?
4. Can you change the punctuation in the following sentence so that it will please feminists rather than insult them? ''Woman, without her man, would be a beast.''
5. What three words, when added to BE, ON, and RE, form three new words?

For all five answers see page 215.

TOM SWIFTIES

During the period when Will Weng was editing the puzzles for *The New York Times,* he published several puzzles by a priest named Father Edward J. O'Brien. The crosswords were humorous parodies stemming from the popular *Tom Swift* novels written by Edward L. Stratemeyer, and perused with fervor by boys in the twenties and thirties. In these books, the hero's statements often contained adverbs. For example, a sentence might read, " 'I'm sorry,' said Tom apologetically."

In later decades, Tom Swifties became a fad. The idea was to connect the adverb with the statement via a pun or some other kind of wordplay. I don't think Father O'Brien invented Tom Swifties, but he certainly gave them a tremendous boost and stamped them with his unique brand of wit. Here are three examples from his puzzles:

"I bequeath," said Tom willingly.

"Maid's night off," said Tom helplessly.

"K," said Tom rationally.

Now I present a challenge to you. The following ten sentences are taken from the O'Brien puzzles, but the adverbs are omitted. See how many you can hit on the head. I've tried them on about a dozen bright people, and the best score was 5. If you surpass that record, go to the head of Father O'Brien's class!

1. "Brothers," said Tom _____ .
2. "Pope," said Tom _____ .
3. "Pass the cards," said Tom _____ .
4. "X's and," said Tom _____ .
5. "Coda," said Tom _____ .
6. "Young M.D.," said Tom _____ .
7. "Zero," said Tom _____ .
8. ". . . and lose a few," said Tom _____ .
9. "Go easy, Mr. Roper," said Tom _____ .
10. "Elec. unit," said Tom _____ .

The following are my own Tom Swifties—possibly not so clever as Father O'Brien's, but probably easier than his. A score of 6 is excellent in this case.

1. "I've been pursued by sexy women," said Tom _____ .
2. "You make me blush," said Tom _____ .

3. "It's an amulet," said Tom _____ .

4. "She's naked!" said Tom _____ .

5. "He was every inch a king," said Tom _____ .

6. "I won the cup," said Tom _____ .

7. "They're on supermarket shelves," said Tom _____ .

8. "He's a fine author," said Tom _____ .

9. "My kite lost the contest," said Tom _____ .

10. "I never sent the package to the poor," said Tom _____ .

Answers to all twenty Tom Swifties appear on page 215.

HI!

The object of this game is to fill in the spaces on either side of each HI and make a six-letter word in each case. You may use any letters of the alphabet except HI. In some instances, you may wish to use the same letter more than once in a single word. Plurals are acceptable, but not proper names.

Note that the letters have point values. I tried to reach a total score of 100, but fell short by 10 points. If you can beat my score, send me your list and I'll reward you with a pat on the back.

POINT VALUES

E, S = 1
A, D, L, N, O, R, T, U = 2
B, C, G, M, P, V = 3
F, J, K, Q, W, X, Y, Z = 4

```
__ H I __
__ H I __
__ H I __
__ H I __
__ H I __
__ H I __
__ H I __
__ H I __
__ H I __
__ H I __
```

See my answers on page 216.

FI!

What better way to be tuned in to words than to have HI! followed by FI! Now you are required to make seven-letter words using any letters except FI.

POINT VALUES

E, H, S = 1
A, D, L, N, O, R, T, U = 2
B, C, G, M, P, V = 3
J, K, Q, W, X, Y, Z = 4

My score was 118. Can you beat it?

```
_ _ _  F I  _ _
_ _ _  F I  _ _
_ _ _  F I  _ _
_ _ _  F I  _ _
_ _ _  F I  _ _
_ _ _  F I  _ _
_ _ _  F I  _ _
_ _ _  F I  _ _
_ _ _  F I  _ _
_ _ _  F I  _ _
```

See my answers on page 216.

TRANSFERS

Using all the letters in the following sentence, fill in the answers to the clues below. A famous quotation will appear as you read from top to bottom.

G. I. HERO'S LAUGHTER IS A MOOD TO MOVE.

1. Prevaricators   — — — — —
2. Auxiliary verb   — — — — —
3. In the direction of   — —
4. Possess   — — — —
5. Satisfactory   — — — —
6. Kahn–Van Alstyne song   — — — — — — — —

If you think the puzzle is too easy, here's a challenge. Create a different sentence from mine, using all the letters in the quotation. If you believe it's too difficult, I have come up with a second sentence that is probably better than the one about the G.I.

See page 216 for my second sentence and the answer to the famous quotation.

Just in case Transfers may intrigue you, here's another one:

THREATEN? BEAT? CRUEL FAULTS!

1. French conjunction   — —
2. "Eri____," Verdi aria   — —
3. Yahoo   — — — — —
4. Subsequently   — — — — —
5. Genesis topic   — — — —
6. Lyricist for Gershwin's "Swanee"   — — — — — —

Again, if the puzzle proves to be too simple, you are challenged to create a better message than mine, using all the letters in the quotation. In this case, I am offering a free copy of my book *Across and Down* to the reader who sends in the best message. As for the solution to the second Transfer, see page 216.

THE HIDDEN WORD

When you have completed this puzzle, circle the first letter of each word. Reading from top to bottom, you will then find a word meaning "persons skilled in pronunciation."

DEFINITIONS

1. He wrote *Pal Joey*   _ _ _ _ _
2. What tenants pay   _ _ _ _
3. Confidence; faith   _ _ _ _ _
4. Incongruous jumble   _ _ _ _
5. Olympic star of 1936   _ _ _ _ _
6. Receding   _ _ _ _ _ _
7. Small stone on the beach   _ _ _ _ _ _
8. Saucy; insolent   _ _ _ _ _ _ _ _ _ _
9. Helot   _ _ _ _ _
10. Silverweed   _ _ _ _ _
11. Book of the Old Testament   _ _ _ _ _ _

Here's a second set of clues for another unusual word. The clues are a bit more "jazzy."

DEFINITIONS

1. Kind of police   _ _ _ _ _ _ _
2. Aladdin's loss   _ _ _ _
3. A Met score   _ _ _ _
4. Source of ear-itation   _ _ _ _
5. He has "I" trouble   _ _ _ _ _ _
6. This bud's for you, America   _ _ _ _
7. Calaboose   _ _ _ _
8. Man in a cast   _ _ _ _ _
9. Black suit   _ _ _ _ _ _
10. Where Daisy would look sweet   _ _ _ _

In the above case, the Hidden Word is a card game. For the answers see page 216.

CRAZY CLUES

Some of the definitions in the above word game remind me that, in an effort to spice up the puzzles that I have been editing for *The New York Times* and *Simon and Schuster's Crossword Puzzle Book* series, I have included here and there some peppery and salty clues.

Here are some samples. If you have tackled the above puzzles in the past, you will recognize the offbeat definitions. If not, you are in for either a trick or a treat.

THREE-LETTER WORDS

1. She raised Cain
2. Sextet in "Little Nellie Kelly"
3. Wright wing
4. He's never out of butts
5. Junior's Saturday evening post
6. Person in a shack
7. Crow's relative
8. Mixer's frozen asset
9. This may be hard to follow
10. Ewe said it

FOUR-LETTER WORDS

1. Where to see the Lincoln Memorial
2. Long-gone politician
3. Fruit for a politician
4. Ballplayer who had lots of spring
5. Child's need
6. Where to put your dough
7. Burned-out tennis player?
8. Boston flyer
9. Some are tight
10. When both hands are up
11. Roads scholar
12. The longest sentence
13. It's sometimes for the birds
14. One way to stand
15. Make the wild mild

FIVE-LETTER WORDS

1. He fails to pass the bar
2. Rod once waving on a court
3. Girl in a pool
4. Garb for an ardent lover?
5. The mating game
6. He has a stable job
7. Kind of driver in a garage
8. An eye-opener
9. World's biggest holdup man
10. His product may be stolen

SIX-LETTER WORDS

1. He has a racket
2. His salad days are over
3. He has pressing problems
4. Man in a box
5. Knighthood?
6. The man with the hue
7. Person in a cage
8. He has vested interests
9. He had a safe occupation
10. What a tired kangaroo is out of

SEVEN-LETTER WORDS

1. Falls for a married man
2. Insurance man's best policy
3. This person has class
4. One who may be a star
5. Where Gloria got sick on

Altogether there are fifty definitions listed above. Now let's see how adept you are at solving Crazy Clues.

40–50   Amazing! You're a *pun*-dit.
30–39   Clever! you're a smart-burro.
20–29   Average: You're not so cunning at punning.
10–19   Sharpen your wits.
 0–9   You should be *pun*-ished.

The answers are listed on pages 216–17.

MATCH GAME

Here are ten pairs of synonyms. Match the words in column A with those in column B. The answers are on page 217.

A.	B.	
1. savant	a. redundant	____
2. planation	b. nimbus	____
3. xyloid	c. theow	____
4. hispid	d. detrition	____
5. gloriole	e. depreciate	____
6. pejorate	f. polyhistor	____
7. malison	g. translucent	____
8. tautological	h. ligneous	____
9. helot	i. anathema	____
10. perspicuous	j. setaceous	____

A score of 8 is good; 9 is excellent and 10 is amazing!

By the way, this game can be played at a party of word lovers. The host should act as referee. Before the guests arrive, the host should consult a dictionary of synonyms or any other lexicon and collect a large list of synonyms. The list is then transferred to 3″ × 5″ index cards, one word per card. The cards are shuffled and dealt and the game may begin.

The host should prepare enough cards to supply each player with six. For example, if four people are playing, twenty-four cards should be prepared.

The object of the game is to match the most synonyms. Each time players match two words that have the same meaning, they place the pair faceup in front of them on the table. The referee decides whether they are valid synonyms. If valid, the pairs are turned over and kept by the players who successfully matched them.

If a player is overruled by the referee, all the others take turns, from left to right, to declare that they have a match with either or both cards of the player who was mistaken.

If correct, the declarer takes the mistaken player's card and turns it over along with the one from his own hand that made a match.

If incorrect, the others take turns trying to match the declarer's card on the table.

As soon as the preliminary matching has been completed, the player to the left of the referee must place one of his or her unmatched cards faceup on the table. Once again, players take turns declaring whether or not they can match the card on the table. The game proceeds as before until all cards are matched or until all players are stumped.

A more complicated, but more exciting, version of Match Game occurs when the host prepares lists of three synonyms. In this case, players must acquire all three before turning the cards down and keeping them.

If you wish to play the host-referee, here are some synonyms from which you may wish to choose two or three in each instance:

1. rotten, putrid, decayed, purulent, rancid
2. harmful, pernicious, noxious, detrimental, deleterious
3. nonsense, balderdash, hogwash, tommyrot
4. clarity, pellucidness, lucency, limpidness
5. bamboozle, hoodwink, palter, dupe, fool
6. panegyrical, eulogistic, encomiastic, laudatory
7. pariah, outcast, expatriate, rejectee, leper
8. scintilla, spark, glimmer, trace, soupçon, gleam
9. farrago, hodgepodge, mishmash, jumble
10. guide, cicerone, leader, coryphaeus, escort
11. torpid, sluggish, lethargic, phlegmatic
12. spurious, counterfeit, fraudulent, imitation
13. rogue, knave, scapegrace, rapscallion
14. boasting, rodomontade, braggadocio, gasconade
15. quackery, cozenage, charlatanism, sciolism
16. oracular, prophetic, sibylic, vatical, divinatory
17. wealth, opulence, riches, fortune
18. scanty, exiguous, meager, sparse, slight
19. bevel, slant, oblique, cant, chamfer
20. virago, shrew, termagant, fishwife, scold

TITLE SEARCHES

In this game, you are asked to find the title of a best-seller book. The clues are sentences or phrases using all the letters in the title and giving a hint to the title.

1. Here's the first one. Find the name of the book by rearranging the letters in the following message: O, ALL METS FEAR WAR.
    To help you out, the title looks like this: __ __ __ __ __ __ __ __ __ __ __ __ __ __ __ .

2. In this Title Search, the book by James A. Peterson deals with the importance of keeping your body sound. Two anagrammatic clues are:
    STEIN LOST FAT
    FAT SET IN: LOST
    The title looks like this: __ __ __ __ __ __ __ __ __ __ __ __ .

3. Now let's take a hit song of 1950 and anagrammatize it. The result is a Cockneyism: 'E LOVE A SIREN. The song looks like this:
    __ __ __ __ __ __ __ __ __ __ __ .

The answers to Title Searches appear on page 217.

Readers are invited to send me their own anagrams for titles of books, songs, movies, etc. The best entry will receive a copy of my *magnum opus,* called *A Pleasure in Words*. Now, that title in itself is a challenge. I can think of WORSE as a starter, but maybe PURSE or PURE would be less hurtful to my ego.

RHYMING CLUES

Since 1950, I have been contributing puzzles to Dell Publishing Company. In the early years, I tried to impress the editors with various techniques. One of them was to rhyme the definitions. Here are ten examples. Can you solve them? The answers appear on page 217.

1. What you'll see
   From the tallest tree   _ _ _ _

2. Something not to do
   When adding two and two   _ _ _ _

3. Beyond a degree,
   Or excessively   _ _ _ _

4. Along with a jack,
   It rides in the back   _ _ _ _

5. This word brings joy
   To a jobless boy   _ _ _ _ _ _

6. A part that's played
   In a thespian's trade   _ _ _ _

7. From where I'm sittin'
   It sure ain't written!   _ _ _ _

8. This abode, I've heard,
   Is the home of a bird   _ _ _ _

9. When you are nervous,
   This may be of service   _ _ _ _ _ _ _

10. This never belongs
    In the listings of wrongs   _ _ _ _

TANGLED JINGLES

Speaking of rhymes, Tangled Jingles is a word game I invented in the 1950s. In most cases, the game involves rhymed elaborations of old and new sayings and other expressions you have often heard. To illustrate, for "An apple a day keeps the doctor away," you might see this couplet:

Baldwin daily goes inside
To foil the other half of Hyde.

At first, the jingle will probably seem senseless to you, but then you may remember that a "Baldwin" is an *apple* and that "the other half of Hyde" is *Doctor* Jekyll. Subsequently the solution should emerge.

In case you need help with the fourteen Tangled Jingles that follow, two sets of clues for each one are supplied on page 217. The answers appear on page 218.

Warning: There are some sesquipedalian words to puzzle you and some tricky puns to add spice to the sauce. The titles, by the way, should help to steer you down the right path.

1. *Bucolic Adage*
   'Tis foolish to enumerate
   The crimson band of Providence
   Before their embryonic state
   Has crystallized to oval rents.

2. *If*
   Should sweet desires burgeon manes
   And prance around the paddock fence,
   Then soon on all the bridle lanes
   Equestrians are mendicants.

3. *And Beware of Greeks . . .*
   This Pegasus that Kringle brought
   May be a worthless mammal;
   Lest expectations come to naught
   Eschew the vision of enamel.

4. *Joe Miller*
   In moonlight whom did you escort—
   What lovely creature of the court?

   You witnessed not nobility,
   but just the better part of me.

5. *The Silent Generation*
   The minor images we rear
   Should be a section of an act,
   And certainly should not appear
   Like sheep or cattle closely packed.

6. *Shaggy Dog Story*
   If you should ever see
   Two boxers lying flat,
   Then take advice from me:
   Go softly as a cat!

7. *Of Lettuce and Cabbage*
   Within your hidden store
   Of necessary greens,
   Are there replacements for
   The star of New Orleans?

8. *Courtier*
   Is there for me this summer day
   While Sol is riding high above,
   Companion for the cage of clay
   Where all begins at love and love?

9. *Advice in an Automat*
   Beware of xyloid circlets, friend—
   Yea, heed me lest you be undone;
   Unlike the gray metallic kind,
   Their score will never come to one.

10. *Manhattan Philosophy*
    This march from dawn to dusk
    Is merely pottery;
    Cerise the globules bask
    In succulent array.

11. *In Any Event*
    Arrive, dominion
    Of king or queen;
    Or approach instead
    The Oxford sheen.

12. *Bitter Rice*
    The easy chair will bring remorse
    To him who apes a Mercury,
    Who follows Venus in her course
    And reaches *relativity*.

13. *Speech Test*
    O donor of the lactic boon,
    With coat the color of the bay,
    I pray you tell me more than soon
    On what you ruminate today.

14. *Old Commercial*
    Oh welcome, Indian befriended!
    Are you stationed, are you mended
    In regard to what will shear
    In sloping arcs from ear to ear?

Tangled Jingles can be played as a party game. The host should supply each guest with five or ten of the above verses and explain the purpose of the game. If a guest is bewildered and needs the clues, the host should show them to that person.

Scoring for correct answers to each jingle is as follows:

10 points for each answer without clues.
5 points for each answer with clues.

The same scoring applies to you if you play the full game alone. Measure yourself as follows:

125–140 points   Genius!

120–135 points   Excellent!

115–130 points   Good going!

110–125 points   Above average

100–120 points   Middling

 95–115 points   Below average

90 points or below—Try some other game.

A variation of the party game is as follows:

The host reads several of my Tangled Jingles to the guests and explains the idea. The host then asks the guests to create original Tangled Jingles, with or without rhymes, using proverbs. The host, in some cases, may wish to supply a list of proverbs.

Here are ten that may do the trick:

1. A miss is as good as a mile.
2. Making mountains out of molehills.
3. Necessity is the mother of invention.
4. A new broom sweeps clean.
5. Love of money is the root of all evil.
6. An ounce of prevention is worth a pound of cure.
7. He who laughs last, laughs best.
8. A fool and his money are soon parted.
9. One swallow does not make a summer.
10. The proof of the pudding is in the eating.

After the guests have created their punny or esoteric alternatives to the various proverbs, the host collects and shuffles their papers before reading them aloud. The guests try to guess each proverb, and later they vote on the best of the lot. The host may wish to give prizes to the best guesser and the best proverb-changer.

CONVERSIONS

This game is featured in many puzzle magazines. You can play it alone or in competition with one or more people. The object is to convert a word into another word by changing only one letter at a time. Here's an example involving opposite emotions—devised by Lewis Carroll.

> HATE
> HAVE
> LAVE
> LOVE

Now, I challenge you to tie or beat me in the following ten instances. The numbers in parentheses indicate the number of steps I took.

1. ARM into LEG (6)
2. RIVER into WATER (4)
3. GIVE into TAKE (5)
4. RAKE into TOOL (6)
5. FISH into BOAT (7)
6. BEAR into LION (6)
7. STAR into MOON (7)
8. HARP into LYRE (5)
9. TREE into CHOP (8)
10. BEAT into FLOG (5)

The answers appear on page 218.

OFF WITH ITS HEAD!

There are hundreds of English words that can be decapitated twice to make new words. An example is SWALLOW. By dropping the first letter, we get WALLOW. And when the initial *W* is omitted, ALLOW pops up.

Here are ten five-letter words that can be decapitated twice to make new words. But instead of giving you the word, I have defined it. I have also defined the words that occur when the first letters are dropped. An example is:

Twenty—center of an apple—native metal

The answer would be:

SCORE—CORE—ORE

Now go to it! The answers are on page 218.

1. Vapid—story—pub drink
2. Box for oranges—appraise—consumed
3. Sword part—put on cargo—fruit drink
4. Seat—growth on the head—atmosphere
5. Weary—angry—carmine
6. Condone—connection—cartoonist's need
7. Asparagus shoot—fruit—sound receiver
8. Fragile—banister—feel sick
9. Carapace—Hades—building addition
10. Tiny—tree-lined walk—entire

Challenge: What seven-letter word can be beheaded four times and end with ATE?

WHAT, NO VOWELS!

Recently after I had given a speech on puzzles to a group of advertisers in Boston, one young account executive asked me to name a common three-letter word that has no vowels.

Naturally, I asked him if I could count *y* as a vowel and he nixed that notion, thus eliminating *try, shy, sky, dry,* etc.

I thought for a few moments and said: "PDQ!" His reply was, "No, acronyms are not allowed. Also, no interjections." I pondered for a few more seconds and finally gave up. When he told me the word, I felt ashamed. Why hadn't I thought of it?

Now, dear reader, can you come up with the right answer? Also, can you tell me what PDQ stands for?

The answers appear on page 218.

Incidentally, I posed the no-vowels question to a Scrabble tournament player and he immediately gave the right answer. He also informed me that there is a less common three-letter word composed of consonants only. It's *cwm* (pronounced *koom*) and it's a geological term meaning, "a deep, steep-walled amphitheatrical recess in a mountain caused by glacial erosion." In case you're interested, it's a synonym for *cirque.*

My Scrabbling friend then went further in his effort to enlighten me on longer no-vowels words. He cited the following:

1. *crwth* (pronounced *krooth*), which is an ancient Celtic stringed instrument and is also spelled as *crowd*
2. *phpht* and *pht,* which are interjections used as expressions of mild anger or annoyance
3. *tsktsk*—to utter an exclamation of annoyance

Cwm and *crwth* are listed in *Webster's Second. Phpht* and *pht* can be found in *The Official Scrabble Players Dictionary* (the lack of the apostrophe is not my fault, and I cannot find the two words in any of my lexicons). *Tsktsk* appears in *Random House.*

The last three words remind me that my adman had eliminated *tsk, phpht* and *pht,* as well as *tst* and *ssh,* when he put the kibosh on interjections. Lest I cause the reader annoyance, I'll now hush-hush on this no-vowel subject.

LIMERICKS

As previously stated, many word games can be played alone or by two people in competition or at a party. Limericks is one of those versatile games. Contrary to popular belief, Edward Lear did not invent this verse form, but he certainly popularized it in his *Book of Nonsense* (1846).

A limerick has five lines, the last of which is a humorous punch line. When played as a game, the last line of the verse is omitted, and the player is asked to supply it. This practice often leads to ribaldry and outrageous wordplay. For example, I give you a limerick of anonymous authorship. The creator of this one resisted the temptation to settle for obscenity, but came up with a delightful pun.

The last line of this limerick, as well as the last lines of the others that follow, can be found on page 218.

> There once was a man from Nantucket
> Who kept all his cash in a bucket;
> But his daughter, named Nan
> Ran away with a man
>
> _____ .

Crossword-puzzle fans have often been treated to original limericks by constructor-versifier Frances Hansen. Here are four of her gems. In each case, try to create a fifth line that rhymes with her first line.

1. *A Toast*
   Now here's to the gentle giraffe;
   She isn't a beauty, by haffe;
      Her neck is too long
      And her odor is strong,

   _____ .

2. *Force of Habit*
   Two rabbits who lived in a hutch
   Grew bored with love-making and such;
      They decided to quit,
      And they did, for a bit,

   _____ .

3. *Dik-Dik*

    At the funeral rites for a dik-dik

    Who had swallowed a clock at a pik-nik;

        The mourners grew nervous

        As, during the service,

    _____ .

4. *Hazy History*

    Some Persians flew into a pet

    With some people named Medes whom they met;

        What the fuss was about,

        Or how it turned out,

    _____ .

P-T FLEET

As a crossword-puzzle constructor-editor, I have often transferred my waking hours into dreamland. Black and white squares float through the air and demand to be filled with words. I create fantastic crossings involving neglected letters like *Q, J, X* and *Z*. But when the alarm clock rudely returns me to the real world, all my amazing crossings vanish immediately like the smiling Cheshire cat.

But a strange phenomenon occurred while I was writing this book. Sometime during my sleep, maybe about 5:00 A.M., I was listing six-letter words that began with *P* and contained a *T* as the fifth letter. Believe me, I am not making this up! My brain held onto the idea when I was released from the arms of Morpheus. I rushed out into the kitchen in my pajamas and grabbed a piece of scrap paper and listed some of the words. As I did so, others occurred to me. Hence, it is a *must* that I include this item lest all the spirits that roam the outer spheres condemn me for spurning their "inspiration."

After some research in *Webster's Third* I have come up with twenty-four words that fill the bill. Some of the words are rather abstruse, but all are legitimate. No plurals are allowed, nor are any proper names. I now challenge you to find ten other words that meet the same requirements as POTATO, POLITE and PALATE.

A score of 11 or more makes you an admiral and 10 gives you a captaincy. If you can find 9, you're a fine P-T commander*, and a score of 8 makes you an ensign. A total of 7 puts you on the boat, but with 6 or below, you sink. Note that *sink* is not spelled with a *T*!

P __ __ __ T __
P __ __ __ T __
P __ __ __ T __
P __ __ __ T __
P __ __ __ T __
P __ __ __ T __
P __ __ __ T __
P __ __ __ T __
P __ __ __ T __
P __ __ __ T __

Some possible answers appear on page 218.

*Did you know that in the U.S. Navy a commander is lower than a captain?

BRAIN GAMES

My colleague Will Shortz has produced three volumes of *Brain Games*, published by Simon and Schuster. He has kindly given me permission to reprint several of his puzzling creations from the first volume.

While scanning the book, I came upon a feast of word games and found it hard to choose one above the other. Finally I settled on the following four teasers.

I. For each number, think of a four-letter word answering the clue in parentheses, and fill it in in the blank *backwards* to complete a longer word.

    EXAMPLE: L ___O C A T___ ION   (Mexican sandwich)
    1. ANT _____ E   (fishing rod)
    2. S _____ ENT   (earth)
    3. FA _____ LL   (pitcher)
    4. BE _____ ER   (face cover)
    5. DI _____ ARY   (small bell's sound)
    6. L _____ ENT   (short skirt)
    7. D _____ ANTE   (television: slang)
    8. PAR _____ ENT   (send)

II. Underline the gemstone concealed in the letters of each sentence.

    Example: Don't <u>rub y</u>our nose if you have sunburn.

    1. Not every M.D. can cure damp ear lining.
    2. Thou shalt rename thy stepchild Antony.
    3. Rubbery legs are no asset for marathons.
    4. Safari men blew clarions to stop a zebra.
    5. The corporal said I am on duty this eve.
    6. A fiery old pinto can gallop a long way.

III. Rearrange each line of words to form a meaningful sentence. No punctuation is needed except the period.

    EXAMPLE: Travelers start a smart head get always.
              <u>Smart travelers always get a head start.</u>

1. To with up kids are some put hard.

    _____

2. This content pancake one morning with yourself.

    _____

3. Two students drew a question on most blank.

    _____

4. My my number five than fingers hand's.

    _____

5. Entrance these have paintings lovely you me.

    _____

6. Beyond medium voices from the heard the.

    _____

IV. Change one letter in each word to make a set of three words often spoken together. Strike the letters you change.

   EXAMPLE: locḱ   stoŕk   barreĺ   _lock, stock and barrel_

   1. slap   grackle   pox   _____
   2. hood   link   sinner   _____
   3. may   roman   chili   _____
   4. rod   while   clue   _____
   5. bun   morn   start   _____
   6. step   loom   listed   _____
   7. reads   wilting   axle   _____
   8. tame   sew   watch   _____
   9. how   slip   rump   _____
   10. bug   sorrow   steak   _____
   11. wind   woken   long   _____

Answers to all four Brain Grames appear on page 218.

PALINDROMES

Palindromists don't aim to puzzle you. They create their phrases or sentences mainly for the satisfaction of finding groups of words that will read the same backward as forward. Also, they strain their brains to gain the acclaim of others, or to give their readers a different sort of enjoyment.

Palindromes have a Greek background, from *palin* (again) and *dramein* (to run). In fact, the ancient Greeks found pleasure in this word game. The satirist Sotades, for example, wrote a palindromic sonnet in the third century B.C. Poor Sotades! His enemies sealed him in a chest of lead and threw him into the sea—but not just because of his sonnet. His many lampoons of public figures brought him a Mafia-style demise.

EVE is one of the shortest palindromes; RADAR and LEVEL are others; HANNAH is a six-letter example.

Most crossword-puzzle fans will recognize the palindromic statement about Napoleon in exile: ABLE WAS I ERE I SAW ELBA.

My personal favorite is A MAN, A PLAN, A CANAL: PANAMA! I wish I knew who created that beauty; but, as in most cases, the palindromist is Mr. or Ms. Anonymous. Incidentally, I wonder whom the author had in mind. Perhaps it was George Washington Goethals, the engineer who brought the canal to completion after Vicomte Ferdinand-Marie de Lesseps had given up because of financial and political problems.

Just as "I—Why?" is considered to be the best of the briefest poems, the first man's first statement to his new mate is a cla ssic. What clever English-speaking person invented MADAM, I'M ADAM? Kudos to him or her!

In that connection, I recently received an advance copy of a new book (copyright 1987) published by Charles Scribner's Sons. The title is *Madam, I'm Adam*, and it contains one fine palindrome after another—all created by a wordsmith named William Irvine. With the permission of the author and the publisher, I quote a few of the gems.

NO EVIL SHAHS LIVE ON.
LAGER, SIR, IS REGAL.
SENILE FELINES
KAYAK SALAD —ALASKA YAK

Mr. Irvine, who has spent a lifetime making words go forward and backward, is not above sexy sentences. For example:

NAOMI, DID I MOAN?
EROS? SIDNEY MY END IS SORE!

But what makes Mr. Irvine's fine work come to life are the illustrations by Steven Guarnaccia. For instance, a woman is shown in some corner of a casino working on a slot machine. The palindrome reads: RENO LONER.

On another page, a missile is depicted dropping down on a group of expressionless nerds standing in a circle. The palindrome reads: BOMBARD A DRAB MOB.

What I like about Mr. Irvine's creations is that they are brief. When palindromists attempt long statements, the meaning gets a bit muddled. Here's an example recently submitted to me: BOSTON ODE: WAIT! RENITENT NOW, BUT NINE MEN IN TUB WON'T NET INERTIA! WE DO NOT SOB.

Excellent try—but is that an ode? And why is Boston involved with nine men in a tub? Maybe the palindromist is talking about the Red Sox, who have been unable to win a World Series for many decades.

Here's a challenge for you from Mr. Irvine. The end of the palindrome is BY DEMOCRATS, and the illustration shows a man dressed as a mule onstage. The answer appears on page 219.

(Please send me your best palindromes. If I receive enough of them, maybe I'll publish my own book—with proper credit and cash to individual authors!)

BRIEF INTERLUDE

Four quickies are presented below. The first two are relatively easy. The third one involves a pun, and you may wish to use it to stump your friends. The last one is not tricky, but it's hard to get.

1. What ten-letter word contains three sets of double letters?
2. What do these letters mean? IMOKRU
3. Here's a strange definition for a common five-letter word: HIJKLMNO. What's the word?
4. What six-letter word contains seven other words without changing a single letter?

The answers can be found on page 219.

REBUSES

When I was a little boy, one of my aunts gave me a Christmas present that I cherished. It contained rebuses relating to famous people. Rebuses, as you probably know, are modes of expressing words and phrases by pictures of objects whose names resemble those words or the syllables of which they are composed.

The first picture in the book showed a woman scrubbing some laundry, and down below was a drawing of a weight marked "2,000 pounds." Proudly, I wrote WASHING-TON at the bottom.

Another illustration depicted a lovely young woman pointing to a Model-T, and the salesman was saying: "Thank you, Mary!" As an avid moviegoer, I wrote MARY PICK-FORD.

Today, a rebus is far more subtle and brief. Illustrations are cut to the bone and puns are rampant. Here are some of my own creations. If you can solve them over all, you have earned the honorable title of REBUSITE.

The solutions await you on page 219.

1. $\dfrac{0}{10}$

2. THER ◊ OUGH

3. $\dfrac{\text{STAND?}}{\text{DO} \quad \text{U}}$

4. $\dfrac{\text{AUTHOR THOMAS}}{\text{CORPORATION BIGWIGS}}$

5. THE π SKY

6. TCHCECPCLCOCT

7. HOR TOWNACE

8. WIRE MEASURE (1) SIMBA

9. RU (CAR) N

10.
```
          H
   S            O
   E            R
          S
```

Dear reader, you are challenged to create your own rebuses for your next gathering of word-lovers. May your imagination exceed your expectation and result in acclamation!

RIDDLES

One of the world's oldest word games is the pastime called riddles. Ever since I was a child, I have loved such silly quizzes. The ones that please me most are those that entail puns or other kinds of wordplay. I still chuckle when I recall that a garbage truck is the answer to "What has four wheels and flies?"

Here are twenty of my favorite riddles. If you can guess half of them, you deserve an honorary degree in enigmatology.

The answers appear on page 219.

1. Why is a tramp like flannel?
2. At what time of day was Adam born?
3. Why are noisy cats like vandals?
4. When does a sculptor make provision for the future?
5. What is the keynote to social graces?
6. If a stove costs $500, what would a ton of coal come to?
7. On what day of the year do bores talk the least?
8. What state is round at both ends and high in the middle?
9. Can you name the oldest settler in the West?
10. When are two apples most alike?
11. Why is a kiss like a rumor?
12. What is the difference between a fisherman and a hooky player?
13. Why are free seats in a church inadvisable?
14. What word of ten letters can be spelled with only five?
15. What men are always above board in their movements?
16. What is taken before you get it?
17. What is it that every man, no matter how clever or meticulous, always overlooks?
18. Why shouldn't the British talk about their queen?
19. Why should men avoid the letter *A?*
20. Why is a pig in a parlor like a house on fire?

Perhaps the most famous example of this genre is the riddle of the Sphinx. As you may recall, the Sphinx guarded Thebes and posed a riddle to all who wished to enter the city. No one could guess it until Oedipus came along. When he gave the right answer, the Sphinx got so mortified that she threw herself into an abyss.

The riddle? "What goes on four feet in the morning, on two feet at noon, and on three feet in the evening?"

The answer, of course, is *man*—a crawler on all fours in the dawn of life, an upright walker in his prime, and a user of a cane in the twilight of his existence.

By the way, "riddles" and "conundrums" are synonyms and both words have taken on broader connotations. In some contexts, they are synonymous with mysteries or any puzzling or difficult problems.

In that connection, you may remember Churchill's famous statement about the USSR in a radio speech on 1 October 1939: "I cannot forecast to you the action of Russia. It is a riddle wrapped in a mystery inside an enigma."

Before leaving the riddles topic, I think it's appropriate to point out that some of the posers do not depend on puns and other forms of wordplay but on clear thinking. Here are three well-known examples that have been going the rounds for many decades. The first calls for some arithmetical skill; the other two demand the use of logic.

The answers can be found on page 219.

1. A frog has fallen into the bottom of a pit that is 45 feet deep. He starts jumping up along steplike rocks. He ascends at the rate of 3 feet each day, but falls back 2 feet every night. How many days will it take him to get out?

2. A man has a fox, a goose and some corn. He wants to take them across a river, but he has only a tiny raft and can take only one of the three at a time. If he leaves the fox with the goose, the fox will have a feast. If he leaves the goose with the corn, the goose will enjoy a meal. How does he get all three across?

    Hint: Assume that the fox will not eat the corn.

3. A prisoner received a visit from another man. After the visitor left, a guard asked the prisoner: "Who was that man? Was he a relative of yours?"

    The prisoner responded with a rhyme:

    "Brothers and sisters I have none,
      But that man's father is my father's son."

    What was the relationship of the visitor to the prisoner?

My friend Barbara Vought has contributed the following original riddles to this section:

1. What plant must contain a number of ounces?
2. What kind of assistance does Les Brown need?
3. How many hot dogs are needed in the dog days?
4. What button doesn't chime when you push it?
5. What makes a furlong?

The answers appear on page 219.

ANAGRAMS

Here is still another game with a long and distinguished history. Like the palindrome, the anagram's etymological background is Greek. Freely translated, it means "letters going backward." Examples of early anagrams are: evil—live, avid—diva. But people soon extended this form of word game to mean any transposition of letters in one word resulting in the creation of another legitimate word. A lengthy example is changing *catechism* into *schematic*.

Anagrammatic tricks crop up in almost every language. Here's one from Latin. Pilate is said to have asked: *"Quid est veritas?"*—translated as, "What is truth?" Some Latin scholar answered with an anagram for his question: / *"Est vir qui adest"*—translated as, "It is the man who is here." When we consider the fact that Jesus Christ was standing before Pilate when the procurator asked his question, the anagram seems to be most apt.

In the Middle Ages, people anagrammatized their own names and the names of others, and mystic connections were made regarding the nature of the person or his possible vocation or fate. Thus, since MALESKA becomes SAM LAKE, I should take up boating or maybe I shouldn't go near the water!

Somewhere along the line, folks developed anagrams into a word game that could be played alone or in competition with others. The game has been marketed by different companies and was one of the best-sellers before Scrabble, Boggle, etc., came along.

What you get when you buy Anagrams is a box of hundreds of letters and a set of rules and directions. However, you can easily make your own letters; all you need is lots of file cards, a pair of scissors and some good sense concerning the distribution of consonants and vowels. For example, you would make many more *E*'s than *U*'s and you would go easy on *J*'s, *X*'s, *Q*'s and *Z*'s.

As for directions, I am grateful to Richard Wilbur, our poet laureate, for the following description. Quotation marks have been omitted because I have made a few editorial alterations.

The letters are turned facedown and spread about the corners of the table so as to be in reach of the players (ideally two, three or four).

Each player draws a tile (or card) and turns it over in the center of the table. The nearest to *A* will begin the play.

Now each player draws a second time, and thus the first player in a game of four persons will have one letter in front of him and four in the pot. Out of the five, he will seek to make a word of three or four letters.

Let's say our first player has managed to spell a three-letter word solely from the letters in the pot. He puts the letter he has drawn into the pot and draws another letter from the fringes of the table. If he can now make a second word, he does so and draws and plays once more. Throughout the game, a player may continue to draw and play each time he makes a new word. A total of eight words constitutes a victory.

When a player can't make a new word but can add to or modify a word which he already possesses, he may do so but must surrender his turn to the person on his left. In doing so, he must put the letter he has just drawn into the pot, if unused, and then must draw again in anticipation of his next turn. He follows the same procedure if he cannot make any move at all.

Once a word has been placed on the table in front of a player, other players can take it away by building on it and changing the root. For example, if CHARM has been made by Player A, one of his opponents cannot take it away by merely adding an *S*. A change from CHARM to MARCHES would be proper.

It is not permissible to combine two or more words belonging to a player even if more words are added.

SOME OTHER RULES AND SUGGESTIONS

Players should agree on a dictionary in advance. If a player makes a word and an opponent feels it's not in the dictionary, the opponent may challenge. If the challenge is upheld, the player who has made the word must break it up, and mix the letters with those in the pot. If the challenge resulted from building on another player's word, the other player's word must be restored and the challenged player must return the letter he has just drawn to the pot. In either case, the challenged player also loses his next turn. If the challenger is wrong, he loses his next turn.

Slang words and foreign words fully adopted into English are permitted. Capitalized words, abbreviations, hyphenated words, obsolete words and dialect are *not* permitted. Words beginning with RE or ending in ER (such as REHATCH or CONSIDERER) are acceptable only if spelled out in the dictionary.

Some people observe a rule that when one player has made eight words he is the immediate winner. Others insist that play must continue until that round is complete before the winner is declared. This second process sometimes results in a tie. At any rate, either procedure should be established in advance.

It should be emphasized that the Wilbur method is just one of many. For example, some people prefer a free-for-all game in which players do not take turns. The one who gets there "fustest with the mostest" usually wins.

Other people continue play for a certain number of turns or until after a time limit has expired, when the player with the most *letters* in front of him is the winner. Thus, a player having four seven-letter words would defeat another who has six four-letter words.

Finally, I should point out that my personal preference is to play Anagrams or any other table game with only one opponent. The advantages are:

1. It's quieter and you can think more clearly.
2. You don't have to wait a long time for your next turn.
3. The table is not cluttered.
4. Superiority or inferiority is more easily determined.

As for #4, my beloved wife (Jean) and I played Anagrams for years and switched to Scrabble in the fifties. In either game, we couldn't resist helping each other. Hence, we never found out who was the better player—and it didn't matter!

WORD RACE

This variation of Anagrams, as well as the next one, was introduced to me by Mary W. McLees. I have played both games with friends and have enjoyed them.

In Word Race, the object is eventually to build ten acceptable four-letter words before the other players do so.

There are four draws from the "boneyard" (all the letters laid facedown on the table). On each draw, players may return a maximum of four of their picks in order to obtain a mixture of consonants and vowels.

Draw 1—Players pick twelve letters. After returns are made, play begins. Each player must make three four-letter words. Any player who cannot do so is out of the game.

Draw 2—Players do not wait for each other to finish the task required above. They proceed to draw eight letters and, after returns, must now make two more four-letter words without touching the words already made. Again, any player who cannot do so is eliminated.

Draw 3—After completing the second draw, each player now picks ten more letters and, after returns, must make two five-letter words without touching the other words. Players who cannot do so are eliminated.

Draw 4—Again, ten letters are drawn. These are combined with the five-letter words and five four-letter words are made.

If none of the remaining players can complete the task, the one with the most four-letter words is the winner.

MAKE AND TAKE

The object of this game is to make the longest words and the most words within a time limit previously agreed upon. It is essentially an abbreviated version of the Anagrams game described earlier.

From the "boneyard" each player draws one letter. The one with a letter nearest to the beginning of the alphabet is the first player, and play proceeds from left to right.

Each player now picks three more letters, one at a time. After four picks, if a player has no vowels, he or she should return one of the consonants. If another consonant is picked, that player loses a turn.

The same rules apply if a player has picked four vowels.

In turn, players begin to make four-letter words. Still taking turns, they pick one letter at a time and try to build on their own words or on the words made by others. In the latter case, the player who builds on another's word takes it and places it in front of himself or herself.

When the time limit is about to expire, the *last round* is declared and the game ends when the last player has completed a turn.

Scoring is as follows:

10-letter word or more	10 points
9-letter word	9 points
8-letter word	8 points, etc.

Note: It is inadvisable to play any Anagrams game with Scrabble tiles because there are not enough letters in the boneyard.

Finally, I wonder what two common words are the longest that can be anagrammatized. Readers are invited to send their suggestions. My nomination is ORIENTALISM. The anagram for that eleven-letter word is printed upside down at the bottom of this page.

ELIMINATORS

THE LICENSE GAME

Whenever Jean and I would take long rides in the car, we would alternate between playing Scribble (see chapter 1) and The License Game.

The rules are simple. You look for a car with a license that contains three letters of the alphabet. Let's say that VBL pops up. The idea is to think of a word that contains those three letters in that order.

The first one to call out a legitimate word gets a point. But suppose I shout "Verbal" and simultaneously my opponent yells "Inevitable." She wins because her word is longer.

If neither player can think of a word, that license is discarded and the search continues for another.

When playing the game alone, I have developed my own scoring system. If a license stumps me, I give *them* 3 points. If I come up with a word, 1 point goes to *me*. This is fair because I'm admittedly a wordmonger. For example, on a recent ride, I scored points on the following licenses:

1.	XGO	6.	PMC
2.	ZMT	7.	MQT
3.	PNJ	8.	YTN
4.	BQY	9.	PBH
5.	PHU	10.	HYL

My words appear on page 219. You may have others that are just as good, and probably better!

FAMOUS INITIALS

When I was a schoolboy, I had a best friend named Billy. Like me, he enjoyed word games. On a hot summer day, we used to sit in the shade of his screened-in porch and play the A, B, C, D game.

Billy: Apple
Gene: Box
Billy: Camel
Gene: Dog

But we discovered that such an unrestricted game was too easy, so we limited the game to categories, such as given names.

Billy: Andrew
Gene: Benjamin
Billy: Carl
Gene: David

But that category proved unsatisfactory when we reached such letters as *Q* and *X*. Neither of us knew a Quincy or a Xavier.

And so, we tried fruits, flowers, cars, etc., but finally we gave up. Without categories, the game was too easy; with them, it was too hard.

One day I told my wife about our frustrating experiences on Billy's porch, and she challenged me to create a new game along the same lines. I retreated to my "think tank" and finally came up with Famous Initials!

The rules are rather simple. The first player must start with a famous person, either real or fictional, whose first name begins with A—for example, Andy Hardy. Now the second player must come up with a first name that begins with B and a surname beginning with I. (The B follows the A in Andy and the I follows the H in Hardy).

If the second player cannot think of a last name beginning with *I,* he or she may settle for merely using the first name. For example, the call might be Benjamin Franklin. No score.

Now the first player must conjure up a famous name with the initials C.G. Let's say that Cary Grant is called. Voilà! The player has zeroed in on both initials and has scored one point.

Now the opponent must think of a name with the initials D.H. Well, how about that famous tennis player, Doris Hart? Excellent! A point for the other side!

It's the first player's turn again, and the required initials are E.I. Unable to match *both* initials, this player chooses Washington Irving—a good play because the opponent is stuck with X.J.!

In this game, it rarely happens that a player cannot think of a name that fits either initial. When that unusual event occurs, the opponent is declared the winner regardless of the number of points previously scored.

Now let me give you just one more example from a torrid game between Jean and me that I have extracted from my files.

> Gene: Alan King
> Jean: Burt Lancaster (1 point)
> Gene: Carol Channing (couldn't think of a surname with M)
> Jean: Doris Day (1 point)
> Gene: Emma Eames (1 point; hooray for opera!)
> Jean: Fred Flintstone (1 point; comics should be barred!)
> Gene: Greta Garbo (1 point)
> Jean: Hedda Hopper (1 point)
> Gene: Ida Lupino (darn those surnames starting with I!)
> Jean: James Mason (1 point)
> Gene: Katherine Hepburn (K-N is a hard combination)
> Jean: Lawrence Olivier (she got stuck on that I!)
> Gene: Mary Pickford (1 point; aha!)
> Jean: Norma Shearer (Got her on that Q surname!)

Well, the game went on until Jean changed my Rudolph Valentino into Paul Williams, the pop singer. Although she scored no points for that move, she cleverly left me with a Q-X combination, which stumped me completely.

By the way, this is another of those games that can be played by three or more people at parties. If you try it and it fails, don't write to me. But if it's a hit, let me know. To quote Clint Eastwood, it will "make my day!"

OLD GLORY

A few years ago two fine wordsmiths spent the July 4th weekend at my home. In honor of the occasion, I invented a game that I called Old Glory, and I challenged my visitors to compete against each other.

The rules are simple. Players take turns calling out phrases or names or titles using *red, white* and *blue* in that order. They are given thirty seconds to think of an appropriate call. If a call is incorrect or repeats one that has been used before, the player loses. Also, he or she loses if the thirty-second time limit has expired.

In the July 4th instance, I acted as timekeeper and referee. What amazed me was that they were able to come up with *sixty* correct calls before one of them gave up.

Here are the first four calls. How many more can you add?

    A. Red tape
    B. White water

    A. ''Blue Skies''
    B. Red herring

It's my guess that the average person will have a hard time reaching a total of *thirty*. Remember that my two friends were experts.

Incidentally, Old Glory can also be played by four, five or seven persons, but never by three or six, because each player would be constantly getting the same color.

The 60 calls made by A and B are listed on page 220.

THE A-A GAME

Every one of the five words listed below contains two A's. Using *all* the letters at the left, build five common nouns.

D, D, D   1. __ __ __ __ __

I   2. __ __ __ __ __

L, L   3. __ __ __ __ __ __

M, M, M   4. __ __ __ __ __ __

N, N   5. __ __ __ __ __ __

P

R, R, R

My answers appear on page 220. You may have other solutions that fit.

WORD ASSOCIATION

On the TV program called "Equalizer," McCall (the hero) sometimes plays Word Association with his aide. Here's an example:

McCall: Chicken

Aide: Chicken Little

McCall: Little Eva

Aide: Eva Marie Saint

McCall: Saint Thomas Aquinas

Since his aide could not think of a phrase or name starting with *Aquinas,* McCall won.

However, my friends and I have developed our own rule for the game. Since it is relatively easy to stump one's opponent, the rule is that the caller must have another phrase or name in mind. Thus, McCall would lose unless he himself could come up with something beginning with *Aquinas.*

This rule serves to extend the game. Callers must reject obvious stumpers. For example, let us say that Joe is playing Bill.

Joe: Short

Bill: Shortstop (Bill rejected *short shrift* because he himself was unable
        to think of a phrase or name starting with *shrift.*)

Joe: Stop sign

Bill: Signpost

Joe: Postmaster

Bill: Masterpiece

Joe: Piece of one's mind

Bill: Mind over matter

Joe: Matter of fact

At this point, Bill could not think of a phrase beginning with *fact.* He challenged Joe, who promptly responded: "Fact-finding," and won the game.

Please note that the above is pure Word Association. No deviations occurred. However, some people prefer to loosen the rules. For example, plurals are allowed. In this variation, Bill could have called: "Facts of life." Another loosening of the rules is to allow the word in question to be placed anywhere in the answer instead of first. For instance, suppose Joe had called: "Matter of course." Bill would have been permitted to respond: "In the course of time." My preference is for the pure version; but any form of Word Association is an enjoyable, mind-challenging pastime.

SENSIBLE SENTENCES

This game was sent to me by Edgar E. Theimer, brother of Ernst Theimer—one of the best crossword-puzzle constructors in America. It's a relatively easy solo game, which I have enjoyed. Also, if duplicated, it can be turned into a party game in which a prize might be awarded to the person who finishes first.

The object of the game is to fit the words in the list into the blanks in the sentence.

1. Did you _____ your _____ in _____ and water to make this _____ turtle _____ ?
   mock, soap, sock, soup, soak

2. I'll bet that _____ _____ _____ a _____ ! Are you headed for the Arctic? All we get here is a light _____ at _____ .
   most, mist, mint, mink, coat, cost

3. _____ _____ played many _____ , but would have been miscast as _____—the loner at every _____ , who wanted to _____ .
   Parks, marry, party, Marty, Larry, parts

4. Come _____ , I expect to be _____ summoned for _____ .
   jury, duly, July, duty

5. It was not a _____ _____ . Galloping Shoes won by a _____ .
   (To make it a bit harder, the list is omitted.)

All answers may be found on page 220.

Popular Commercial Word Games

Scrabble leads the pack and is here to stay regardless of its faults. As most word lovers know, the game was invented by architect Alfred Butts in the 1930s. He called it Lexico and sold a small number of sets to friends. Among those friends were Mr. and Mrs. James Brunot, who realized the commercial possibilities of the game and began to put together sets in their home in Newton, Connecticut. They also changed the name to Scrabble.

Only a few thousand sets were sold until 1952 when the owner of Macy's happened to play the game. He was so delighted by it that he told the manager of the toy department to stock it. Sales zoomed and the word got around to other stores. At that point a New York company, Selchow & Righter, which was making the boards for the Brunots, bought the rights to Scrabble and subsequently made millions of dollars.

Various forms of Scrabble are played in different languages throughout the world. Tournaments are held, and in America the contestants memorize the words in *The Official Scrabble Players Dictionary,* published by Merriam-Webster, Inc., and copyrighted by Selchow & Righter. The lexicon contains over 100,000 entries, ranging from two-letter words to eight-letter words.

Some of the two-letter words are *ae, ai, li* and *xu.* In the three-letter list, one finds *aal, fud, kef, kif, pyx,* etc. Four-letter words include *gald, goph, xyst* and a host of others that a good crossword-puzzle constructor would hesitate to use.

When Scrabble became somewhat popular in the fifties, my wife and I bought a set and played the game night after night. Our goal was to try to beat our own record for the highest combined score. Also, we kept an account of how many "rack-cleaners" (called "bingos" by tournament players) we could put on the board in a single game.

On 1 August 1958 we reached our pinnacle—a score of 1,163, including seven "rack-cleaners." After playing 150 games, we made some tabulations and found that our median combined score was 815. Also, the highest individual score was 662. These figures may sound startling to the average Scrabble player, but it should be stressed that we helped each other in every game rather than using strategies to prevent a triple score by one or the other.

In those days there was no *O.S.P.D. (Official Scrabble Players Dictionary)*, hence, when one of us would find it necessary to use a two-letter word like *ka*, we would consult our Webster's unabridged dictionary. If the word was listed, we would write it in ink on one of the borders of the board. After the first hundred games our board was littered with esoteric two-letter words!

Aside from the abundance of abstruse little words, another fault we found with Scrabble was the frustration of finding all vowels or all consonants on our racks. Most of the time we stubbornly refused to give up a turn in order to replace some of the letters.

I have since discovered that many amateur Scrabble players separate the vowels and consonants prior to the game and choose a mixture. I wish Mr. Butts had chosen that method. It would have increased successful moves and decreased the feeling of bafflement.

A third problem that has often cropped up in the games I have played is the extreme disappointment of discovering a seven-letter word on my rack and finding no place to put it. This usually happens toward the end of the game.

Still another grievance of mine is the lack of fluidity. Unlike Anagrams or even Boggle, once the letters are placed on the board they remain fixed in that position. After awhile, I get sick of staring at certain sections upon which it is impossible to build.

Finally, Mr. Butts and the Brunots should have been more scientific in their distribution of letters. As just one example, there is an overabundance of the letter *I*.

Having said all that, I still think Scrabble is a fascinating game and it will do until a better one comes along.

Finally, here's an item on the 1987 international Scrabble contest. It appeared in the *St. Petersburg Times* on 10 July 1987.

V-I-C-T-O-R-Y SPELLS $5,000

LAS VEGAS, Nev.—Rita Norr, of New York City, defeated 340 top Scrabble players and claimed $5,000 cash for first place in an international competition.

"She became the first woman in the history of organized Scrabble competitions to win the event," said John D. Williams, director of Scrabble Players, Inc., an organization that governs the 200 Scrabble clubs and 12,000 members in the United States and Canada.

"An interesting point is that people actually go into training for the event by studying word lists, playing endless matches against computers and running and doing aerobics to increase stamina," Williams said.

During the competition, which Ms. Norr won Wednesday, players endure play of up to six games in one day, with an expert averaging 400 to 500 points per game, Williams added.

Ms. Norr has been playing seriously for about seven years. "I don't remember being good at spelling bees," she said.

Boggle, in my opinion, is the best rival of Scrabble. In this game, produced by Parker Brothers, players shake lettered cubes in a tray and then try to create words from the exposed letters. They may move in straight lines or diagonally, or they may follow a zigzag course from cube to cube.

I especially like Big Boggle because it affords the opportunity to put together long words. Another pleasing aspect of the game is the fact that it's not static. If the players don't like what they see, they give the tray a shake and presto—a whole new set of letters appears.

My only quarrels with Boggle are that I feel confused and I'm not used to going up, sideways, down and diagonally while creating a word. In contrast, I feel comfortable with the horizontal positions of the words in Anagrams.

Incidentally, the above criticism reminds me that I detest Word Search and other games of the same ilk having different titles. In Boggle, at least I'm creating the words; in Word Search, I'm slavishly finding the entries hidden by someone else among lots of *x*'s and other little-used letters.

Razzle is another Parker Brothers game that, to the best of my knowledge, never gained wide popularity. It uses a board that looks like a football field or hockey rink. The idea is to spell enough four- or five-letter words to back your opponent against his own wall and score a point.

The problem with Razzle is that you are working with only five letters for each play. That's too confining for people like me.

Ad-Lib, manufactured by E. S. Lowe Company, is a takeoff on Scrabble. The big difference is that the point values are on the board rather than on the tiles. My wife and I bought the game and found it to be a rather welcome change from Scrabble.

But the color of our board was a dull, drab, depressing brown; also, the tiles were so fancy that we sometimes had trouble distinguishing one letter from another. These criticisms reveal the importance of packaging.

About twenty years ago, Selchow & Righter spent a lot of money advertising on television a game called R.S.V.P. Somebody bought me the game for my birthday. My wife and I played it about ten times and relegated it to the cellar.

R.S.V.P. features a sort of stand-up screen with slots for lettered cubes. One player sits on one side of the screen and the opponent is stationed on the other side. They take turns fitting letters into the slots to make words. In so doing, they often block the other person. For example, if my wife created WATCH, the word would appear backward on my side. What could I do with HCTAW?

We also found fitting the letters into the slots to be a tedious job, and it bothered us to have a screen between us—like prisoners peering through cell bars.

Word Rummy is a game produced by a company called Gabriel. Its greatest advantage is that it's low-priced. The game is similar to my Word Poker and, therefore, to me, has a limited appeal. To enjoy it, you must be a word lover who likes to play card games.

Another deficiency is that good players make so many combinations that the table becomes overcrowded with cards that are laid down.

Probe is a Parker Brothers game using lettered cards. The players secretly select cards that spell out whatever words they have in mind. The cards are placed facedown in card racks in the proper spelling sequence. The object of the game is to guess the opponent's secret word by calling out letters. When a letter that appears in the secret word is called, the opponent must turn over that letter.

The above is an oversimplification of Probe. Many people find the rules too long and too complicated. Personally, I would rate it B + .

Among the many games produced by The Milton Bradley Company, I like Jeopardy! most. Like the popular TV program, the answer is given and the object is to guess the question. For example, in a tray under a plastic cover are various categories such as ''Singers,'' ''Democrats,'' ''Television,'' etc.

Under ''Singers'' one answer might read: ''Astaire's famous partner in 1945; she earned the eighth highest salary in the United States.'' The question, of course, is ''Who is Ginger Rogers?'' If Jeopardy! is played as a party game, the first person to shout out the question earns points.

One minor problem is that devotees of the game run out of items and must send away for another set of answers and questions. But that keeps Mr. Bradley happy!

In that connection, here's an interesting anecdote. My wife, our daughter, our son-in-law and I spent a rainy weekend playing Jeopardy! Eventually we had exhausted all the items in our edition of the game. So we decided to write questions and ask for the answers. Our son-in-law announced that his category was "Unusual Geographical Places." He then read aloud question 1:

"What creek in Louisiana was named for a British general who opposed Washington?"

After thinking a few moments, I shouted: "Howe's Bayou!"

Our son-in-law smiled. "I'm okay! How's by you?"

Truthfully, I should not have included Jeopardy! in this list because it is a test of knowledge and speed rather than a word game. But it's such a fine game that I couldn't resist it.

In view of the above, I suppose I should mention Selchow & Righter's Trivial Pursuit, which actually outsold Scrabble when it first hit the market. I hear that it was invented by former professional hockey players. If so, I'm startled and delighted simultaneously. I admire hockey players for their amazing athletic skills, but I always thought that their encyclopedic and linguistic abilities were on a par with their competency in pugilism.

I have no idea as to the worth of Trivial Pursuit, because I have only played it once. A neighbor brought it to my house but left the board at home because he thought it was irrelevant. I did well on sports and opera and he excelled me in the areas of movies and botany. We ended up in a flat-footed tie.

News has reached me that Trivial Pursuit and its many imitators are novas—blazing stars that fade as fast as they brighten. Be that as it may, Mr. Fred L. Worth has certainly capitalized on the fad. Knowing that I'm a crossword-puzzle editor, sundry friends and relatives have gifted me with four of his books: *The Trivia Encyclopedia* (hard cover) and Supertrivia *I, II* and *III*. The value of Mr. Worth's books I do not know. I try to avoid delving into them lest the crosswords get clogged up with a plethora of inconsequential esoterica.

Have I omitted your favorite commercial word game? In that case, I offer my apologies. The above is all I know and, perhaps, all I need to know.

Acrostics

Acrostics deserve their own niche in this book because they are so long-lived, so popular and so unique.

There are several types of acrostics dating back to the period before Christ lived:

1. A composition, usually in verse, in which the first letters of each line spell out a word, a name, or a phrase.
2. A word made from any of the letters in the words of a phrase (this form is similar to an acronym such as NATO).
3. A "word square" in which the words read horizontally and vertically. An example is:

```
H E A R T
E M B E R
A B U S E
R E S I N
T R E N D
```

All of the above word games were played by the Romans and continued to be popular through the centuries, especially in England and France. Among American writers, Edgar Allan Poe took great interest in acrostics.

Today, acrostic puzzles are the rage, and most of the credit for their success goes to Elizabeth Kingsley, who invented the name Double-Crostic and copyrighted it. Her innovation was to embody a literary quotation in the puzzle.

Thomas Middleton is the present guru in the acrostics field. He was kind enough to contribute the following history of the Double-Crostic, along with some helpful hints on how to solve one. (I have deliberately omitted quotation marks.)

Double-Crostics first appeared in *The Saturday Review of Literature* in the early 1930s. They were created by Elizabeth Kingsley and very quickly became favorites among such members of New York's literary set as the regulars at the Algonquin Hotel's "round table." Shortly after their first appearance in *SRL,* Mrs. Kingsley was asked to do them for *The New York Times* also. Then Simon and Schuster inaugurated their series of D-C books, all original puzzles, all by Mrs. Kingsley, who was followed as the *Times* Double-Crostician in the late '40s by Doris Nash Wortman. I succeeded Mrs. Wortman in either '66 or '67.

A Double-Crostic is always based on a quotation from a published work. The author and title of the work are spelled out as an acrostic: the first letters of the clued Words, as you read down, will give you the author and title. The numbered letters in the clued Words, transferred to their corresponding spaces in the diagram, will spell out the quotation. If there is no black square at the end of a line in the diagram, the word will be continued on the succeeding line.

An exciting feature of these puzzles is that they are, in a sense, organic. You can work not only from the Words to the diagram, but back again from the diagram to the Words. If, for instance, you see

22 G	23 J		24 Z	25 M	26 O		27 B	28 Z		29 L	30 W		31 X	32 C	33 P		34 Q	35 H
I			W		S		A			F			S	H			
36 M		37 D	38 K	39 S	40 Y	41 K		42 T	43 V	44 U	45 D						
D		N		E	R			B		E							

you might readily guess that the entire phrase will prove to be "IT WAS AS IF SHE HAD NEVER BEEN . . ."

The little letters in the upper left-hand corners of the squares in the diagram tell you which Words those letters came from.

I doubt that there is a puzzlehead in the United States who hasn't on occasion finished the big crossword puzzle in *The New York Times Magazine,* all except for one or two or three or four little squares that he just can't be sure of. One advantage of the acrostics is that, except on very rare occasions, once you begin to see patterns forming in the diagrammed quotation, a flood of excitement sets in, and in time your pencil (or pen, if you're that secure) starts to fly from Words to diagram and back, and the puzzle gets completed. Very seldom does one *almost* complete one of these puzzles. Once you're on a roll, you're pretty sure to achieve total success.

Bear in mind that many, many thousands of people complete these things with great regularity, so, no matter how formidable they may appear at first, or even second or third, glance, they are solvable by determined puzzleheads.

Give it your best shot.

Mr. Middleton has submitted an acrostic from one of his Simon and Schuster books. The answer appears on page 221.

CLUES

WORDS

A Essence; phantom; zeal ....
<u>17</u> <u>3</u> <u>85</u> <u>140</u> <u>176</u> <u>12</u>

B Dominating ....
<u>125</u> <u>84</u> <u>158</u> <u>6</u> <u>190</u> <u>187</u> <u>131</u> <u>62</u> <u>174</u> <u>52</u> <u>141</u>

C Dutch colonial administrator in America (1580-1638) ....
<u>107</u> <u>156</u> <u>90</u> <u>25</u> <u>7</u> <u>50</u>

D Aberration ....
<u>69</u> <u>154</u> <u>45</u> <u>35</u> <u>82</u> <u>110</u> <u>137</u> <u>119</u> <u>57</u> <u>160</u> <u>18</u> <u>2</u>

E Without aim or purpose ....
<u>33</u> <u>79</u> <u>124</u> <u>95</u> <u>139</u> <u>186</u> <u>142</u> <u>53</u>

F Thick slices ....
<u>162</u> <u>182</u> <u>104</u> <u>149</u> <u>173</u>

G Optional ....
<u>92</u> <u>134</u> <u>70</u> <u>24</u> <u>144</u> <u>66</u> <u>34</u> <u>46</u>

H Large-billed tropical American bird ....
<u>172</u> <u>181</u> <u>61</u> <u>38</u> <u>49</u> <u>76</u>

I Minute dipterous insect ....
<u>54</u> <u>115</u> <u>30</u> <u>86</u> <u>183</u>

J Predetermined, arranged, set ....
<u>98</u> <u>60</u> <u>114</u> <u>111</u> <u>81</u> <u>109</u> <u>27</u> <u>32</u> <u>71</u>

K Aberrant ....
<u>133</u> <u>41</u> <u>161</u> <u>153</u> <u>118</u> <u>64</u> <u>99</u> <u>122</u> <u>26</u>

L Heartache ....
<u>42</u> <u>97</u> <u>185</u> <u>78</u> <u>22</u>

M Female red deer ....
<u>106</u> <u>87</u> <u>56</u> <u>159</u>

N Semilegendary fabulist ....
<u>89</u> <u>108</u> <u>113</u> <u>189</u> <u>151</u>

O Manager of the Yankees, 1931-46 ....
<u>167</u> <u>105</u> <u>121</u> <u>37</u> <u>152</u> <u>120</u> <u>1</u> <u>138</u>

P Intimate association or relation .....
<u>91</u> <u>16</u> <u>94</u> <u>184</u> <u>40</u> <u>83</u> <u>143</u> <u>128</u> <u>126</u> <u>9</u>

Q Intentional slight; insult ....
<u>178</u> <u>21</u> <u>112</u> <u>165</u> <u>168</u> <u>59</u> <u>145</u>

R Gull with a very short or rudimentary hind toe ....
<u>39</u> <u>23</u> <u>103</u> <u>155</u> <u>10</u> <u>179</u> <u>96</u> <u>129</u> <u>136</u>

S Faint illumination on the part of the moon not lit by the sun ....
<u>102</u> <u>73</u> <u>36</u> <u>135</u> <u>180</u> <u>63</u> <u>48</u> <u>20</u> <u>68</u> <u>150</u>

T Feels, discerns ....
<u>80</u> <u>65</u> <u>147</u> <u>11</u> <u>14</u> <u>177</u>

U Assistant ....
<u>58</u> <u>132</u> <u>188</u> <u>75</u> <u>67</u> <u>51</u> <u>74</u> <u>175</u>

V Sap, dolt, numskull ....
<u>171</u> <u>117</u> <u>123</u> <u>29</u> <u>148</u>

W Cut into small cubes ....
<u>19</u> <u>44</u> <u>5</u> <u>130</u>

X Wife of Hector and mother of Astyanax ....
<u>28</u> <u>31</u> <u>101</u> <u>116</u> <u>146</u> <u>15</u> <u>93</u> <u>77</u> <u>13</u> <u>166</u>

Y Bathes ....
<u>88</u> <u>164</u> <u>43</u> <u>170</u> <u>8</u>

Z Emanation from the body of a medium ....
<u>100</u> <u>157</u> <u>47</u> <u>4</u> <u>163</u> <u>127</u> <u>55</u> <u>72</u> <u>169</u>

					1 O	2 D	3 A	4 Z	5 W	6 B
7 C	8 Y	9 P		10 R	11 T		12 A	13 X	14 T		15 X
16 P	17 A	18 D		19 W	20 S	21 Q	22 L	23 R	24 G	25 C	26 K
27 J		28 X	29 V	30 I		31 X	32 J	33 E	34 G	35 D	36 S
37 O	38 H	39 R	40 P	41 K	42 L		43 Y	44 W	45 D	46 G	
47 Z	48 S	49 H	50 C		51 U	52 B	53 E		54 I	55 Z	56 M
	57 D	58 U	59 Q		60 J	61 H	62 B	63 S	64 K	65 T	
66 G	67 U		68 S	69 D	70 G	71 J	72 Z		73 S	74 U	
75 U	76 H	77 X	78 L	79 E	80 T	81 J	82 D	83 P		84 B	85 A
86 I	87 M	88 Y	89 N	90 C	91 P	92 G		93 X	94 P	95 E	
96 R		97 L	98 J	99 K	100 Z		101 X	102 S	103 R	104 F	105 O
106 M	107 C	108 N	109 J	110 D		111 J	112 Q		113 N	114 J	115 I
116 X	117 V	118 K		119 D	120 O		121 O	122 K	123 V	124 E	125 B
126 P		127 Z	128 P	129 R	130 W		131 B	132 U	133 K	134 G	135 S
136 R	137 D	138 O		139 E	140 A		141 B	142 E	143 P	144 G	145 Q
146 X	147 T	148 V		149 F	150 S		151 N	152 O	153 K	154 D	155 R
156 C	157 Z	158 B	159 M		160 D	161 K		162 F	163 Z	164 Y	165 Q
166 X		167 O	168 Q	169 Z	170 Y	171 V	172 H	173 F		174 B	175 U
	176 A	177 T		178 Q		179 R	180 S	181 H	182 F	183 I	184 P
185 L	186 E	187 B		188 U	189 N	190 B					

Crossword Puzzles

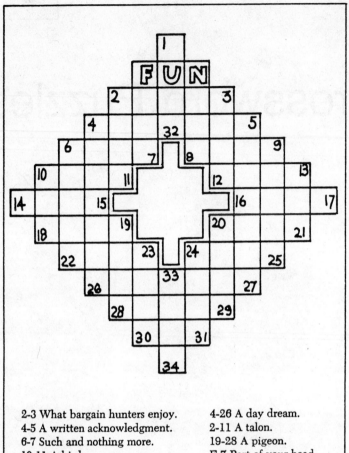

2-3 What bargain hunters enjoy.
4-5 A written acknowledgment.
6-7 Such and nothing more.
10-11 A bird.
14-15 Opposed to less.
18-19 What this puzzle is.
22-23 An animal of prey.
26-27 The close of a day.
28-29 To elude.
30-31 The plural of is.
8-9 To cultivate.
12-13 A bar of wood or iron.
16-17 What artists learn to do.
20-21 Fastened.
24-25 Found on the seashore.
10-18 The fiber of the gomuti palm.
6-22 What we all should be.

4-26 A day dream.
2-11 A talon.
19-28 A pigeon.
F-7 Part of your head.
23-30 A river in Russia.
1-32 To govern.
33-34 An aromatic plant.
N-8 A fist.
24-31 To agree with.
3-12 Part of a ship.
20-29 One.
5-27 Exchanging.
9-25 To sink in mud.
13-21 A boy.

Maybe I'm prejudiced, but I consider crossword puzzles to be preeminent in the field of word games. According to the statisticians, at least fifty million people agree with me. Solving crosswords is the most popular indoor pastime—surpassing such games as bridge, chess, checkers, bingo and poker.

There are many variations of crossword puzzles. In this chapter, samples of selected types will be presented. The solutions are presented on pages 221 to 224.

As most fans know, Arthur Wynne invented the crossword puzzle in 1913. At that time he was the editor of the Fun page in the *New York World Sunday Magazine*. He called his innovation "Word Cross." Mr. Wynne's creation was rather crude. He inserted the word *FUN* and did not number it. Then, throughout the puzzle he gave two numbers for each word. Also, he repeated a word—*DOVE*—a practice shunned by good constructors today. Finally, he placed four "unkeyed letters" in the corners of his diagram.

Despite its shortcomings, the puzzle gained immediate popularity. Hundreds of word lovers submitted their own creations. Soon afterwards Mr. Wynne found it necessary to turn over the job of editing the puzzles to a young woman named Margaret Petherbridge, who had recently joined the staff after graduating from Smith College.

Miss Petherbridge, who subsequently married publisher John Farrar, led the way in evolving the rules for modern American crossword puzzles. More about that will be related later in this chapter. Meanwhile, opposite is Mr. Wynne's Word Cross, reproduced as it originally appeared. The answer is on page 221.

In the 1920s crossword puzzles became the rage, somewhat like the recent Trivial Pursuit fad. Naturally, people who were adept at solving wondered if they were among the best and the brightest. And so, inevitably, crossword contests sprang up.

The first contest was held at the Ambassador Hotel in New York City on Sunday, 18 May 1924. About three hundred people competed in solving an 11×11 puzzle constructed by F. Gregory Hartswick, a close associate of Margaret Petherbridge Farrar.

The winner of the contest was William Stern II, who was then dubbed "Crossword Puzzle Champion of the World." His solving time was 10 minutes, 10⅖ seconds.

Here's the puzzle. Again, please note that there are eight "unkeyed entries" (letters that do not simultaneously fit into a horizontal word and a vertical word). Also, the puzzle contains four two-letter words—a practice frowned upon by most top editors and constructors today.

It's my guess that modern crossword tournament winners could easily solve Mr. Hartswick's challenge in fewer than five minutes. At any rate, I suggest that you consult a watch or a clock and see if you can beat the 1924 champ. The answer is on page 221.

ACROSS

1 Baffle
5 Inflamed
9 Model
11 Exclamation
13 Type of horse
14 Italian river
15 Upper portion
17 Japanese coin
18 Negative
19 Places
21 Lachrymose
23 Form of pastry
24 Negative
25 Coin
27 Concede
29 Skill
30 Pronoun
32 Sherbet
33 Part of "to be"
34 Ass
36 Preposition
37 Violent storm
39 Displays
40 Work for

DOWN

1 Crosspieces
2 Above
3 Indicate systematically
4 Asks
5 Substitute
6 Notwithstanding
7 Preposition
8 Black wood
10 One
12 Troughs for grain
14 Colonnade
16 Place

18 Woman in Bible
20 Numeral
22 Finish
25 Twos
26 Possessive pronoun
27 Hanging
28 Tight
31 Vase
34 Weapon
35 Elegiac poem
37 Directional preposition
38 Alternative conjunction

Incidentally, if you desire to learn more about crossword-puzzle contests, past and present, a chapter on that topic appears in my Simon and Schuster book entitled *Across and Down: Inside the Crossword Puzzle World.*

Many skeptics predicted that the crossword-puzzle craze was just a "flash in the pan." But Margaret Farrar's reply in 1984 was, "If so, it was the longest flash in history."

It is true that the madness subsided in the depressing thirties, but most newspapers published daily puzzles (usually size 13 × 13) and the *New York Herald Tribune* led the way with a daily 15 × 15 puzzle and a large 23 × 23 on Sundays. That newspaper also published cryptograms under the crossword puzzle, and I contributed several. The payment was only $1 per cryptogram, but the big thrill was to see one's name in the paper.

Simultaneously in the early forties I began to submit daily puzzles to the *Trib*. I probably should be entered in the *Guinness Book of World Records* for the most rejections. The total equaled two score before I finally scored in 1943!

Ladies and gentlemen (trumpets blare offstage), here is the first crossword puzzle ever published by Eugene T. Maleska. It appeared in the *New York Herald Tribune,* without prior notification to me, on a sunny 4 August, 1943.

I was driving my father's old car. My bride, who loved puzzles, asked me to stop at a stationery store so that she could buy the *Trib* and solve the daily puzzle while we were riding. When she returned to the car, she immediately opened the paper to the page where the puzzle was printed and she gasped.

"Gene," she shouted, "the puzzle is *yours!*"

I had already put the car in motion, but when I heard those wonderful words I got so excited that I could hardly control the wheel. Finally, I managed to pull over to the curb and take a look. There it was! "Today's puzzle by Eugene T. Maleska." The thrill of that moment is comparable to the first time you make love. It took me fifteen minutes to smoke my pipe and get my nerves into a calmer state before driving off again.

Since that day, I have published over 5,000 puzzles, but now it's old hat even when a large company pays as much as $1,000 for one of my creations. By the way, I received a check for $5 for *numero uno*.

ACROSS

1 Not of the clergy
5 Tooth
10 Roof
14 Egyptian dancing-girl
15 Old-womanish
16 Scent
17 Corded fabrics
18 Saving
20 Rubbed out
22 Windflowers
23 Contends
25 Ireland
26 Catkins
28 Dealer
32 Cot
34 Spanish lariat
36 Monumental slab
37 Opera solo
39 Garb
41 Mythical shield
42 Speaks imperfectly
44 Narrow bands
46 Dine
47 More profound
49 Famous Egyptian statue
51 The bees
53 Most closely related
56 Scattered
60 More meager
61 Not pertinent
63 Scarlett O'Hara's home
64 Color of a horse
65 Hindu princess
66 Aural
67 Condiment
68 Curl the lip
69 Lease

DOWN

1 Household gods
2 Air-raid signal
3 Make perfectly happy
4 Ali Baba's brother
5 Angry
6 Unit
7 Feminine name
8 Put in a row
9 Turn back
10 Crown
11 Scandinavian god
12 Johnnycake
13 Units of energy
19 Turkish princes
21 Always
24 Begin
27 Exhalation
29 Corrupt
30 Lamb

31 Nap
32 Hairless
33 Famous canal
35 Quivering
38 Visible
40 College half-year
43 Calyx leaf
45 Break short
48 Additions to bills
50 Speaker
52 Ninth Hebrew month
54 European songbird
55 Expanse
56 Male titles
57 Malay sail canoe
58 Spoken
59 Staff
62 Born

Solution on page 221.

I have included the preceding puzzle in this chapter partly out of vanity and partly because puzzle fans have often asked me what kind of crosswords I created when I started and how long it took me to make them up. In answer to the second question, I must emulate Colonel Oliver North. "If I recall correctly, it took me eight hours to put that puzzle together."

How long would I take today, after fifty-five years of experience? Probably a half hour, not counting the job of typing the definitions.

On the subject of clues, please note the brevity of many of my definitions in the 1943 puzzle. For example, "Scent" for ODOR and "Ireland" for ERIN. Today, I might define ODOR as "What carbon monoxide lacks" or "What anosmic people don't sense." As for ERIN, today's clue might read "Leprechaun's land" or "Milesian's home."

The above points out one of the differences between a good puzzle today and a crossword in the thirties and forties. In the distant past, editors preferred primary definitions. This caused a repetition of the same clues for the same words. The result was what I call a "knee-jerk" response from solvers. An ODOR was always clued as a "Scent" and a TREE was defined as a "Woody plant." In the end, the excitement involved in solving crosswords was numbed.

Luckily, some Young Turks like Jack Luzzatto and Herb Ettenson came along and persuaded editors to let them fly. For instance, Mr. Luzzatto defined BEE as "Nectar inspector" and Mr. Ettenson's clue for POET was "Meter man." I chipped in by defining NEST as "Nutcracker's suite" and NOON as the outrageous "When both hands are up."

This breakthrough, encouraged by several young editors and by Margaret Farrar, helped crosswords to experience a renascence.

Finally, please note that my first puzzle was typical of those that were published in the first four decades of crosswords. There was no theme! My main entries had absolutely no relationship to one another.

Another important improvement in crossword puzzles occurred in the 1950s when Mrs. Farrar permitted multiple-word entries. I was given the honor of having the first *Times* puzzle of that nature put into print. Across the middle of a daily crossword I featured HARD-SHELLED CRAB. This revolutionary step led to the use of phrases such as ONCE IN A BLUE MOON, titles of books and movies and full names of famous people.

Eventually themes were introduced into the puzzles. At first, they were quite straightforward. For example, the title of a Sunday puzzle might be "Indian File" and the diagram would be filled with the names of tribes or chiefs.

Then along came a clever constructor named Harold Bers. He introduced a new wrinkle into thematic puzzles. Mrs. Farrar dubbed it the "inner-clue" method. Actually it was a form of wordplay. The theme of the Bers opus was, of all things, cigarettes! If memory serves me correctly, CHESTERFIELDS was defined as "Overcoats." What's "A fortunate bowler's coup?" It's a LUCKY STRIKE, and "Ships of the desert" becomes PACK OF CAMELS.

Since the Bers innovation, constructors have been vying with each other in creating all kinds of "inner-clue" puzzles with ingenious titles. But, of course, some popular themes were often repeated. Here's an example. The solution appears on page 221.

ACROSS

1 Artist Chagall
5 Word with white or fire
9 To and ____
12 Discernment
17 Flower part
18 Wayfarer
20 Compute
21 With no unnecessary risks
23 Total
24 "Night ____ a thousand eyes. . .": Lyly
25 Doubleday
26 Followers of novel and social
27 Cinderella's "godmother"
28 In extreme degree
30 Identical response
31 Determinate quantity
32 Milton or Beverly
33 Sissy
37 "____ for Two"
40 Earth inheritors
41 Alone on stage, as a diva
42 Salt Lake City athlete
43 Chinese dynasty 207 B.C.–A.D.220
44 Book jackets
48 Metric measure
50 Pointed instrument
53 College founded by Henry VI in 1440
54 Hair ornament
55 Lift
56 Greek letter
57 Siestas
58 Temporary calm
59 Severe
60 Pair incorrectly
62 Theatrical ploy
64 Invented
66 Sides
67 Toward the sheltered side
68 Beget

69 Curved knife of the North
70 Make up for
71 Body sac
73 Capital of Calvados
74 Graceful tree
75 French mental-health pioneer
76 Change speed
78 Episcopate
79 Mil. address
80 "____ a Rose"
81 Grant of Hollywood
85 Vetch
86 Chaminade piano piece
90 Shakespearean character or man's slipper
91 Recipe direction
93 Mariposa or calla
94 ____ skittles
96 Khaki cotton twill
97 "The ____ Love"
98 Museum offering
100 ____ Anne de Beaupré
101 Tosses
102 Rialto event
105 Flat-bottomed boats
106 Spinal-column segment
107 Moves unsteadily
108 Prefix with mix or mingle
109 Words of assent
110 Italian wine center
111 June honorees

DOWN

1 Scarlett's sweet rival
2 Peter or Paul
3 Ethiopian prince
4 Scours
5 Quarrier's quarry
6 Comedian Johnson
7 "The Cowardly Lion" actor
8 Second person
9 Corpulent

10 Pack away a second time
11 Worthless leavings
12 Lessee
13 Middle of a Neil Simon comedy
14 Fail to address problems head-on
15 Conservative
16 Compass dir.
17 Disunion
19 Expel
20 Say no
22 Recipe meas.
29 Wapiti
30 Make into law
33 Falstaff's pal
34 High mountain
35 Relating to hearing
36 "____ Magic"
38 Abalone
39 Dill of the Bible
41 Spot for a slalom race
44 RBI's, e.g.
45 Most unctuous
46 Canton in W Switzerland
47 First name in mystery lore
48 Closely trimmed
49 Convex moldings
50 Furnish with weapons
51 He wrote "Maud Muller"
52 Get taken to the cleaners
53 Coating
59 "____ Johnny!"
61 Lion's pride
62 His: Fr.
63 Slave
64 Pepys' claim to fame
65 "____ spiro, spero": S.C. motto
67 Loathe
68 Ascend
70 Church section
72 "The ____ of defeat"

CLOTHES LINE by Jeanette K. Brill

76 Baden-Baden
77 Ref. book
79 "Hands ____ the Sea"
   (Sousa)
81 Heart, to Hadrian
82 Stored up
83 Classified listings
84 Warbles, Tirolese style
86 Marni Nixon is one

87 Spread outward
88 Spanish money
89 Inclined to one side
90 Impede
92 Color slightly
94 Adherent of certain
   religious movement
95 Palindromic conjunction
96 The Campbells, e.g.

97 CCLI × VI
98 Spheres
99 Jaunty
101 Group once headed by
   J.E.H.
103 "From ____ to
   shining. . ."
104 Cartoonist Gardner ____

PUZZLE CUM PUNS by Arnold Moss

ACROSS

1 Fashion item with culottes
6 Organization of "families"
11 Doll Tearsheet, et al.
16 Wedding in Brno?
18 Left bank hat
19 Nude in Novgorod?
20 Glowing
21 Food fragment
22 Well-known stadium
23 "Nyet," in a way
25 "Winnie ____ Pu"
26 Notable nickname in TV
28 Author of "Life With Father"
29 Skinned, as a whale
31 Fish or cut ____
33 Greenland Bay
35 Give too little
38 Position once held by Caesar
40 Gaucho's rope
44 "Wieviel ____ ist es?" (What time is it?)
45 Aria from "Manon"
47 Court character
48 Drink for "enfants"
50 Phoenician fertility goddess
52 Whetstone
53 Status of Whittier's boy
55 Creator of the March family
57 Negative prefix
58 Power source
59 Name of a kind
60 Sluggish
62 What some smokers do
64 Where Ibsen held sway

66 Roman general, in Shakespeare
69 Barnyard sound
70 Circular form
74 Biblical abbr.
75 Army cops
77 Egg
79 Ceres, e.g.
80 Scene of social doings
82 Sight for Minnehaha?
85 Medicinally used poison
86 Quick escape, in Isfahan?
87 Scatter
88 Ford antique
89 Little girl

DOWN

1 Fish favored in Boston
2 Clear sky color
3 Gets the better of
4 School for lts.
5 "____ above all. . ."
6 Great white sharks, e.g.
7 "The Stag ____"
8 Shakespearean word of annoyance
9 ____ instant
10 Ornamental clasp
11 Business degree
12 Give new surface to wood in Helsinki?
13 Seed coverings
14 Uncle Miltie
15 Bucephalus, e.g.
17 Muslim spiritual leader
24 "A right jolly old ____"
27 ____ Saud

30 Where Queenstown was
32 One of five: Abbr.
33 Clam or mussel
34 Wood of the sandarac tree
35 Some Filipinos
36 Choir specialty
37 Spring up
39 Small military group
41 Attuned
42 Placido, for one
43 "____ You Glad You're You?"
46 The same: Lat. abbr.
47 Kind of set
49 O-O, in Bangkok?
51 Useless
54 Present prefix
56 Sesame
59 Filling station device
61 Cain's place of refuge
63 Relative of haw
65 Bathhouse of a kind
66 ____ belli
67 "Stand you awhile ____": "Othello"
68 ____ heating
69 Idaho city
71 "I Get ____," popular song: 1951
72 Coal beds
73 Founder of the "Saturday Review of Literature"
76 Prune a tree, in Ayr
78 Relative of Mr. in Metz
81 Part of many place names
83 Ph.D.'s
84 Year in reign of Antoninus Pius

Still one more deviation from the early no-nonsense puzzles was Mrs. Farrar's introduction of punny crosswords—a form of fun later pursued with vigor by Will Weng during his tenure as *Times* puzzles editor from 1969 to 1977.

Above is an example of a paronomasian puzzle created by a well-known Shakespearean actor-director. The solution can be found on page 222.

Encouraged by fans' delighted reactions to variety in the Sunday puzzles and in the *Simon and Schuster Crossword Puzzle Book* series, Margaret Farrar allowed the rebus idea to pop up in the black and white squares.

Fans were asked to draw stars, flags, ampersands, etc. In that connection, when I succeeded Will Weng as *Times* editor, I inherited an Easter puzzle by Frances Hansen. In the puzzle, sovlers had to draw an Easter egg whenever the letters E-G-G appeared in a row.

One clue was "Skater Fleming" but the diagram contained only three boxes for the answer! It so happened that a sister of the owner of the *Times* was an avid crossword fan. When she couldn't fit PEGGY into those three boxes, she called up her brother and expressed concern theat the "new editor" had made a terrible error! Several phone calls later, the misunderstanding was straightened out and my new job was saved.

Here is an example of a rebus crossword. The solution appears on page 222.

PENNIES FOR YOUR THOUGHTS by Marjorie Pedersen

ACROSS

1 Arthropod
7 Price or Lopez
11 Cookery meas.
14 Song of joy
19 Landing, in Genesis
20 Pope: 1198–1216
22 Word of surrender
23 German "mark"
24 ____ Mazaca, ancient name of Kayseri, Turkey
25 Until now
26 Los Angeles team
27 ____ arms (indignant)
29 Salad ingred.
30 King or Norman
31 Anagram for able
33 "La Vie ____"
36 Green
39 Hobgoblins, e.g.
42 Hawaiian hawks
43 Soul, to Suzanne
44 One-term president's nickname
45 "Lean" one
46 Inst. at Troy, N.Y.
47 ____ green (insecticide)
49 One ____ million
50 Peron or Gabor
51 Junkers-87 (dive-bombers)
53 Crystals
54 Asian holiday
55 Simon or Diamond
57 Imposing
58 Unrefined
59 Ernie or Howard
60 White-tailed eagles
62 Manage barely
64 First twin
66 Where the "Million-Dollar Baby" sold china
73 Expression of regret
74 Tests
75 Chartered
76 Hound, e.g.
79 Consequence
81 Lamp for vaporizing
84 "____-Tin," hit song of 1938
85 Dress-up jacket
86 Some trackmen
87 Cheerless
89 "Piece" for a hood

90 Diff. in every way
91 Robert and Alan
92 Brown, of the "Band of Renown"
93 Tolerate; endure
95 Powerful union: Abbr.
96 Donate, to Burns
97 U.K. flyers
98 Decreases
99 Methane hydrocarbon
101 "____ Fideles"
104 City on the Oka
105 Eye part
106 Twaddle
107 Kind of skirt or bus
109 Lighter
113 Boa
115 ____ fluid
118 He suits his customers
120 Highest peak in Mongolia
121 Focus
122 Stimulus
123 Curved roll or bun
124 Midpoint, to a Londoner
125 Osculate
126 Something hard to beat

DOWN

1 Monster, part horse
2 La Douce
3 Item to be read
4 Steno's needs
5 Female desc.
6 Famous last words
7 Triumphant word
8 Empty
9 Navigational dir.
10 Musical patchworks
11 Wearies
12 ____ Perilous
13 Newscaster Lindstrom
14 Sir Galahad's quality
15 Neighboring, in poetry
16 Unconventionality
17 What "love conquers"
18 He wrote "The Wall Street Gang"
21 Mexican coins
28 Skip
30 Exhibiting cold light
32 Island wreaths
34 Pinches

35 Louis XIV, e.g.
37 Group of speakers
38 Make joyful
39 Play starter
40 Spelunker's interest
41 "Able to corrupt ____ Falstaff
43 Gone up
46 Noisy ones
47 Babbling ones
48 Rhine feeder
52 Ukrainian capital
53 Popular cheese
56 "Merry Widow" composer
58 "I have taken great pains to ____": Shak.
59 ____ over on (fool)
61 Salt, in St. Cloud
63 Merits
65 Rowan
67 Related groups
68 Tristram's lady
69 Ferrara's nobility
70 Marjoram
71 Prepare to travel again
72 Piaf and Cavell
76 Unflinching one
77 Hundredfold
78 Give many details
80 ____ culpa
82 Maine campus
83 Painful bone condition
86 Superb
87 Skillful
88 Olden times
92 ____ Palmas
94 Fenwick and McIntosh
97 Taciturn
100 Tapestry
101 Breastplate
102 "For whom the bell tolls" original source
103 Exudes
108 Chills
110 Dismounted
111 Shift
112 Ins. payment
113 Pod
114 TV type
115 Stress
116 Sphere
117 Greek letter
119 Some

The diagramless puzzle was invented in the 1920s by one of Mrs. Farrar's colleagues, F. Gregory Hartswick. It happened by chance. Someone had sent him a crossword, but he had lost the diagram. Undaunted, he proceeded to re-create the diagram by solving the clues.

My first wife, Jean, solved all my puzzles without diagrams. It wasn't really difficult because most of the puzzles were perfect squares. In contrast, most diagramless puzzles have unusual patterns with lots of open spaces. The first word Across sometimes appears at the far right of the diagram instead of the usual top-left position. As a result, solving a diagramless puzzle is comparable to putting a jigsaw puzzle together. You get helter-skelter groups of words and finally you see how they all fit together.

Diagramless puzzles scare away lots of regular solvers; but once they get the idea and complete one, they are hooked! In my opinion, aficionados of this sort of crossword are the most rabid fans.

If you have never solved a diagramless puzzle and wish to learn, Dell Puzzle Publications' editors have given me permission to reprint their guidelines. Here they are!

HOW TO SOLVE DIAGRAMLESS CROSSWORDS

A MEANS ACROSS; D MEANS DOWN

Three or four "lost" pages in Dell's puzzle magazines because you don't know how to solve the diagramless puzzles? Now's your chance to join the Diagramless Club. Sure, you're eligible. The people who turn first of all to the diagramless aren't any smarter than you—it's just that they've learned the knack of doing those crosswords without the black squares. Like any other skill, it takes a bit of practice, but today we'll get you off to a flying start. You take it from there.

Start with 1-Across, which is ARAB. We've given it to you, but even if we hadn't you could tell it was four letters long, because the next definition is numbered 5-Across. Put a black square at the end of ARAB and at the end of *every* word you write across or down.

Before you go any further, write in 1, 2, 3 and 4 above the letters in ARAB. Always write in the numbers as you go along. They're about the most valuable clues you have—wait awhile and we'll show you why.

Now you've got the initial letters for the first four words Down. The definition for 1-Down is "add to." Try ANNEX there, and don't forget that black square at the end of the word. 2-D, "cook meat by dry heat," is probably ROAST, so you can write that in. 3-D, "re north polar regions," must be ARCTIC, and 4-D, "wager," is BET, we'll bet. Both words go into the diagram, and a black square goes at the bottom of each one.

Where now? Well, all the diagramless puzzles in Dell's puzzle magazines are symmetrical. That is, if you cut the diagram in half diagonally you'll find the pattern in the bottom half mirrors the pattern in the top half. You can notice this in regular crossword puzzles.

ACROSS	DOWN
1 Desert-dweller	1 Add to
5 Noisy breathing	2 Cook meat by
6 Writing tool	dry heat
9 Make into law	3 Re north
10 Past	polar regions
11 Young bear	4 Wager
14 Repose	5 Withered and dry
15 A set procedure	6 Partake (in)
17 No longer existing	7 The "self"
20 Lowest point	8 Part of speech
21 Bobwhite	11 Apple drink
23 Measure out	12 Combine
24 Label	13 Basque cap
27 Implied	16 Scotch cap
29 Soak, as flax	18 Negative
30 Fairy-tale monster	19 Applaud
32 Airplane driver	22 Pale green
34 Coronet	24 Complete
36 Forfeit	25 Nimble
40 Forage plant	26 Money for crooked
42 Female horse	officials
43 Permit	28 2000 pounds
44 Make lace	31 Period of time
45 Spring month	33 Meddle
46 Short poem	35 Female voice
47 Royal	37 Slow, in music
48 Walked	38 Group of three
	39 Shout
	41 Passing fashion
	45 Skill

It is a great help to remember this and to start plotting the lower right of the puzzle as soon as you establish any of the upper left-hand corner. Then when you get to that part you'll know the length and place of the word you'll need. Not only that—you can start solving from the bottom if you get stuck at the top.

Next step. Where does 5-A go? It is defined as "noisy breathing." The problem is, will you put it to the right of 1-A or below it? Check with the Down list of definitions. There is a 5-D, so 5 must begin both an Across word and a Down word. But look again. If 5-A were at the top of the diagram, then its letters would be the initial letters for as many down words. Look at a regular crossword puzzle. You can see that each letter-square in 5-A would have a number, and the next Across word would have to be something like 10-A or 11-A. In this puzzle we're solving now the next definition is 6-A. Therefore, 5-A will have to go *under* 1-A. A look at our start tells us that an S put before NORE gives SNORE—a good word for "noisy breathing."

When an Across word and a Down word both start from the same square we call the letter that goes into that square a "keyed letter." 5-A and 5-D start from the same letter.

5 is a keyed letter, but 6 is also a keyed letter, so there are no Down words from word 5 except the one from the "s" in "snore."

But after 6-A you have 9-A in the definition list, so that means that there are Down words from all the letters of word 6-A. You have keyed letter 6, and then two more Down words (7 and 8) before you come to the next Across word, which is 9.

9 is the next word Across, but it is not keyed, because there is no 9-D in the definition list—no word coming down from 9. However 11 *is* keyed. The definition list contains both 11-A and 11-D. After 11-A the next Across word is 14, so you know that 12 and 13 go down from letters in word 11-A.

We suggest going through the definition list first and circling each number that keys both Down and Across words. Not only is that a double help in thinking of the correct word, but even if you get the Across word with no trouble at all, it's a reminder that you have the initial letter for a Down word.

Word 5-A is in its proper spot. What help is that? It gives you the first letter to 5-D. The definition is "withered and dry." When you've put down SERE you'll see that there is an unkeyed word, ENACT. Another unkeyed word, REST, is below it. Check the definition list again for Across definitions that these words fit. 9 and 14 are right.

Sherlock Holmes isn't necessary to help you find out some facts about 6-A. First, you know it must start on the same row as 5-A. Next, you know it must be three letters long, to take care of numbers 6, 7, and 8. That must be so because you already have 9-A written down.

In what square will you start 6-A? Will you skip one, two or more squares? Take a chance. In solving diagramless puzzles you have to take chances once in a while, but don't let that throw you. If you make a mistake you'll see it very soon. So let us start 6-A just one square over and write PEN. Number the letters, and proceed as before.

If you get stuck with the beginning of a diagramless, knowing that the puzzle is symmetrical, you can start at the bottom and work up.

Note that your last Down is 45. It is a key letter because it is in both Down and Across columns in the definition list. Go in one square and count back four squares. That is because the first word of the puzzle is 4-letters long. Count up three, because BET is 3-letters long and corresponds in position to this section of the puzzle. The definition for 45-D is "skill." The best three-letter word for that is ART. And 45-A is "spring month" in five letters, so APRIL fits in there.

Looking back over the end of the definition list of Across words you find the second one back is "royal." You have a letter R in ART. It obviously must be REGAL. Now you have two words ending in L. You look back over the list and you see 39-D, "shout." YELL fills the bill, so write it down, put a black square above it to show the beginning of the word, and there's another bit of the corner for you.

SUMMARY AND HINTS

- Always number.
- Keep checking definition list for clues.
- Keep plotting the other half of the puzzle.
- Remember the importance of keyed letters.
- Most diagramless solvers use quadrille paper to solve diagramless puzzles. This is paper which is ruled off in squares on both sides of the sheet. You can probably buy a pad of it at your local stationer.
- To become skilled, work a few diagramless by turning to the solution as often as you must. Never mind if it isn't "cricket."
- Your errors will pop out at you, and soon you'll be able to seal up the answer section of the book.

  Here, then, is your start. Take it from here. *You* may be surprised to find you're becoming a diagramless fan—but we won't be. As diagramless devourers from away back, we'll just grin and say, "We told you so!"

The solution appears on page 222.

Somewhere along the line, a constructor (whose name I cannot recall) decided to embody a familiar quotation in a crossword. I liked the idea because such a puzzle would give the solvers the same "bonus" as an acrostic. In 1965 I persuaded Simon and Schuster to try this innovation, and a year later the first volume of *Simon and Schuster's Crossword Book of Quotations* was published. The books continued through Series 17 in 1984.

A good puzzle of this type does not break up a word at the end of a horizontal line. Also, it contains the source of the quotation and the author.

In the following example, there is no single author. Hence, that feature is omitted. The solution appears on page 222.

CONCISE ADVICE by Mary Virginia Orna, O.S.U.

ACROSS

1 Pulitzer Prize novelist Margaret ____ Barnes
5 Westernmost point in U.S.A.
9 Slight distance
13 "Blow wind! ___ wrack!": Macbeth
14 Charmion's companion
15 Arezzo's river
16 **Start of the quotation**
19 Kierkegaard, the Danish philosopher
20 Yuletide message
21 Solesmes season
22 Word with horse or house
24 Devastated
26 Docs
29 Compartments at terminals
31 **Middle of the quotation**
33 Colorless: Comb. form
37 Nastase of the courts
38 Regulus' constellation
39 "____ Christie," O'Neill play
40 ____ energy
42 Feudal tenant
44 Dairy cattle of India
45 Cubic measures
47 "I Want ____," starring Susan Hayward
49 Appropriate
50 Bloke
53 Nickel-copper alloy
54 Philippine tree
56 Trireme accessory
57 Learn: Scot.
58 Slaughter of baseball fame
59 **End of the quotation**
62 Fastidious one
64 ____ judicata
65 University administrator
68 Actor James
70 Chemical suffix
71 Year in the reign of Henry IV of H.R.E.
73 Adagio, e.g.
77 Source of the quotation
80 Emulate Sam Prescott
81 Chief god of Memphis
82 Slangy suffix
83 Kind of legal document
84 Kind of flight
85 Kind of number

DOWN

1 Personates
2 Nautical refrain
3 Ruler in Kuwait
4 Library-request verb
5 End
6 Long-distance communication
7 Relative of an enchilada
8 Escorted to the door
9 Tree feature
10 Wooden objects
11 Distaff kin
12 Snooped (with "about")
17 Hillock
18 Aspersion
23 Future fish
25 Majorca or Minorca
26 Relative of a chassé or a fishtail
27 Centering device
28 Long, thin blade
30 Claire's joint
32 ". . . the meed of some melodious ____ ": Milton
34 MIT graduate
35 The cosmos
36 Neglectful
41 ____ hall, at camp
43 Benedictine title
46 Bathing accessories
48 Idle about
51 Bern's river
52 Bigwig at school
55 Nile denizens
60 Souchong, e.g.
61 Kin to Terpsichore
63 Branches
65 Puppeteer Bil
66 Free
67 Novelist Charles
69 Lear's fivefold lament
72 "____ each life. . .": Longfellow
74 Pure and simple
75 Seagoing vessel of Malaya
76 Drachma fraction
78 Commanded
79 Greek ar

1	2	3	4		5	6	7	8		9	10	11	12
13					14					15			
16				17					18				
19						20					21		
			22		23			24		25			
26	27	28		29			30						
31			32							33	34	35	36
37						38				39			
40				41		42			43		44		
45					46			47		48			
49				50		51	52		53				
54			55		56					57			
58					59			60	61				
			62	63							64		
65	66	67				68			69				
70				71		72			73		74	75	76
77			78					79					
80					81					82			
83					84					85			

When Margaret Farrar published my first Stepquote in the Sunday *Times,* the reactions of the fans were so numerous that the entire section of Letters to the Editor was devoted to the cries of joy, anger, and mystification concerning this strange creation.

Today the same situation exists. Some people hate Stepquotes; others love them. By the way, among the latter group is actor Joseph Cotten. Because of his passion for Stepquotes, he and I have been pen pals for over twenty years.

At any rate, here's an example. The solution appears on page 222.

STEPQUOTE by Eugene T. Maleska

In this puzzle, the quotation drops down like a staircase from left to right.

ACROSS

1 **Start of the Stepquote**
7 Clammy
11 Leaper over Luna
14 Go to extremes
15 What anosmic people don't sense
16 It's between Miss. and Ga.
17 Subject of a Kant critique
18 Behaved or downgraded
20 Reveal one's fallibility
21 Drip-dry material
23 Attractive gal
24 Bandleader Shaw
26 Relatives of umbrettes
27 "___ Nome," Verdi aria
29 **Stepquote: Part III**
31 Antonym for abhor
32 ". . . but ___ cigar is a smoke": Kipling
34 Not so fresh
36 Navigators' concerns
38 Worker for a colony
39 Colleague of Boomer
43 Ending for any of four directions
44 Brought forth some future parrs
47 Hero of "Giants in the Earth"
48 Swabs
50 Fuss and feathers
51 Act like Lydia Languish
53 Solicitous people
56 "John Brown's Body" poet
57 Pub game
59 **Stepquote: Part V**
61 Villa d'___ at Tivoli
62 Teach or Kidd
63 Japan's most important port

65 Yawning
66 Between Arthur and Doyle
68 ___ Kippur
71 Bound
73 Souvenir from Sonora
75 "___ was going . . ."
76 Bestow excessive affection
77 Hardened or accrued
78 Peter and Paul: Abbr.
79 Prognostication is his vocation
80 **End of the Stepquote**

DOWN

1 "The ___ I See You," 1945 song
2 State in no uncertain terms
3 Lead a wild life
4 B. & O., etc.
5 "___ Want to Set the World on Fire": 1941 song
6 **Stepquote: Part II**
7 "Wonderland" bird
8 Gulf of ___, arm of the Arabian Sea
9 Apple-pie maker
10 Go before
11 Author of the quotation
12 Liquid fat
13 Walks in a creek
19 Dawn
22 Optician's product
25 Parsnip or ginseng
26 Neckwear for Dobbin or a desperado
27 Rod who swings a mean bat
28 Where to buy an olpe

30 **Stepquote: Part IV**
33 Hôtel ___ Invalides, Paris
35 First name of Abe's first love
37 In short supply
40 Tells a tale, old salt style
41 One of St. Thomas Aquinas' principles
42 Crest in the Dolomites
45 Cousin of a smash
46 New member of the "400"
49 Escapade
52 Look through a keyhole
54 Ministers to
55 Noun suffix
57 "Reader's ___," source of the quotation
58 One of a swashbuckling trio
60 **Stepquote: Part VI**
62 S.A. rodents
64 Concerning
66 Whale
67 Stettin's stream
69 Cartel in Islam
70 Native of Ecbatana
72 Dactyl or hallux
74 ___ de la Paix, Paris

One of the most difficult puzzles I have ever tried to create is what I call a Slide-Quote. In this kind of crossword, the quotation starts at the top-left and slides down diagonally to the bottom-right.

The Slide-Quote is an offshoot of my invention called Diagonogram, which encompasses a phrase or name instead of a quotation. My first Diagonogram appeared in the *New York Herald Tribune* on 1 November, 1943. The patriotic message that slid down diagonally was: "Trust war bonds."

Here is a typical Slide-Quote. The solution can be found on page 223.

ACROSS

1 Keep ___ on (watch closely)
5 Rapper at the bench
10 Fenway Park thrillers
16 Double exclamation of dismay
17 Bradshaw ploy
19 Foo yong, e.g.
20 Where to see an albatross
21 Seated, like Cordero
22 Tebaldi or Scotto
23 Strait between New Guinea and Australia
25 "___ Been Working on the Railroad"
26 Sense, in Saarland
28 Small bird
29 Start of an O'Neill title
31 Punishment for illegal parking
32 Highly glazed fabric
33 Unseld of the NBA
36 Do an inside job
37 Song from "Strike Up the Band"
38 Blacksmith
39 Main courses in U.S.
41 Get ___ the ground floor
42 Where to hear fans buzzing
43 "In face a lion, but in heart ___"
44 Join a book club
46 Like heavy literature
47 Spot for a board man
48 Crucifix
49 Newman's "Apologia pro ___ Sua"
50 Late stepfather of John-John
53 ___ Yisrael, Jewish homeland
55 Is all agog
57 Source of the quotation
59 Tenor Goeke
60 Priestley's "Johnson ___ Jordan"
62 Pictorial presswork, for short
63 Cry like a baby
64 Betty of songdom
65 House or hall of an estate
66 ___ man, blaster at a quarry
67 Russian council
70 Perspicacious

71 Role for Flynn or Fairbanks
73 Oneness
74 Mozart's "Coronation ___"
75 Actor in "Dragnet"
76 Sounds from a dentist's office
77 Actor Merrill
78 Pugilist's weapon
79 Permeable by liquids
81 City in Oklahoma
82 Reagan's running mate in 1980
83 Houston or Snead
84 Places to look for antiques
88 Extreme difficulties
90 Osmium or argon
93 Turkish VIP
94 Indulges in cabotinage
95 Theologians
96 Hatchetman or muscleman
97 "___ Rides Again"
98 Bit of poetry
99 Relative of a gigolo

DOWN

1 Exactly
2 Charlie Chan's expression
3 Man from Johannesburg
4 Archaeologist's find
5 Something to step on
6 Dhoti, to Gandhi
7 Panache
8 Border lake
9 "And every goose a swan, ___": Kingsley
10 Met mezzo-soprano
11 Straw in the wind
12 Fischer moves them
13 Euphoric feeling
14 What Pele and Orr did in the '70s
15 Ancient Greek coins
17 Star with a tail
18 Injury
24 Sniggler for wrigglers
27 Tabard or Wayside
30 Made a gusset or godet
31 What Gratiano wished to play
32 Dry up, as lips

33 He goes "pop!"
34 Tolerate
35 Music lover's prized possession
37 Pickwick Club poet
38 Cut of halibut
40 Fissure
41 Shipment to Bethlehem
42 Unit in Tracy Austin's game
45 Roulette bet at Monte Carlo
46 ". . . discontent, ___ , disobedience": Burke
49 Presidential prerogative
50 Saracen's milieu
51 Somewhat cold and damp
52 Arms of the Atlantic
54 Salinger's "Franny and ___"
56 Like an anchoret
58 Charon's ferry fare
61 ASPCA doctor
64 "The ___ of Sleep," Kipling poem
65 Fog's fellow traveler
66 First time onstage
67 Granulated
68 Stopped ___ (braked fast)
69 Termagants
70 Cleansed
72 Vessels under Tirpitz's command
74 Prefix with fire or match
75 "The ___ Room," best-seller by French
78 Meticulous; fastidious
79 Mountainous region in central Asia
80 Parties for men only
82 Rabbit or Fox
83 Golfer Ballesteros (Masters winner in 1980)
85 Jean Kerr's "How ___ to Be Perfect": 1978
86 Cabbage, in Cannes
87 Colorado's Great ___ Dunes
89 He was a Giant at 16
91 Actress Ullmann
92 Dolley Madison, ___ Payne

SLIDE-QUOTE by Eugene T. Maleska

Reading diagonally from top-left to bottom-right, you will find an Islamic aphorism.

Always searching for new ways to embody a quotation in a puzzle I invented Circles in the Square. After publishing several of this type myself, I allowed others to get into the act. The following is a fine example by a talented Floridian. The solution is on page 223.

ACROSS

1 Lawful
6 Pelts
11 Paddle
16 Heath
17 Fanon
18 De Valera
19 Eminent
20 German painter (1887–1914)
21 Parasite
22 Spanish variety of cordial flavoring
23 Pliant
24 Author of the quotation
25 Cap-a-____ (from head to toe)
26 Arrow poison
27 Partner of caboodle
28 Lamprey's cousin
29 Rapture
32 Crow's nest, for one
34 What SRO implies
35 See 63 Across
40 Stick
43 Guinness or Waugh
44 Second generation Japanese-American
45 Swerve
46 Hebrew letters
49 Rung
50 French pronoun
52 Canadian prov.
53 Kindled
55 Tennessee Williams play: 1953
57 Contend
58 Interdictions
59 George Bernard Shaw comedy

63 Quotation source, with 61 Down and 35 Across
66 Rune equivalent to "W"
67 Marshall____
69 Sun. talk
70 Alcove
72 Eva Marie
73 Wander
74 Muslim supreme being
75 Unit of fineness for gold
76 Harbinger of spring
77 French____ (AWOL)
78 ____ ear, and. . .
79 Aviator Balbo
80 Sweetened the pot
81 Relative of a canine
82 Primary

DOWN

1 Delaware Indian
2 In contrast to what is literally stated
3 Selma and Florence
4 Frosty desserts
5 Small boy
6 Corn product or Oklahoma town
7 Steamed, in a manner of speaking
8 Famous name in fashion once
9 Actress Sommer
10 Observe
11 Incitement to insurrection against lawful authority
12 Whittle down
13 "That's ____," 1953 song hit
14 Present occasion

15 Use a prie-dieu
23 Tilted
24 Inexpensive cigarette in India
27 Ship akin to a yawl
30 In that respect
31 Bring to public notice
32 Chemical compound
33 Marooned
35 River rapids in a gorge
36 "____ Song Go out of My Heart"
37 Nick was his master
38 Enlarge holes before caulking: Var. sp.
39 Exclamation of surprise or fright
40 Opposite of sans in Savoie
41 Author Mazo ____ Roche
42 Wherry wheel
47 Moses' older brother
48 Scholar
51 Shelter in the north
54 Half of a sawbuck
56 Five of these make 54 Down
59 Lope's cousin
60 Feature in some maps
61 See 63 Across
62 "They ____ long, the days of wine and roses": Dawson
63 Musical syllables
64 Traubel or Reddy
65 Acclaim
67 Word of mouth
68 Climbing plant
71 Roof overhang
72 Mens sana in corpore ____
73 French roast
75 Stanley or Hunter
76 Discharge from military service, informally

CIRCLES IN THE SQUARE by Jeanette K. Brill

In this puzzle, the circled letters from left to right, starting on the top line and moving down line by line, form the quotation.

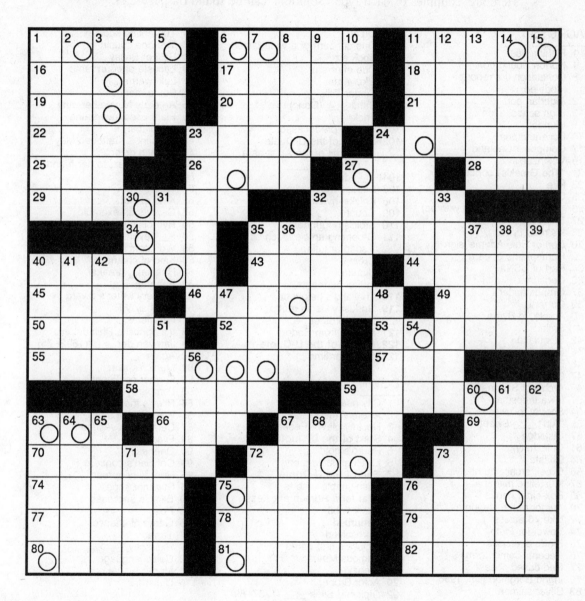

Two other variations of quotation crosswords are the U-Quote and the Boxquote. For the invention of such deviations from the norm, I take the credit or the blame.

Here are examples of each type. Solutions can be found on page 223.

ACROSS

1 Fishing float
4 Norton Sound port
8 Donaldson the reporter
11 Modeled
12 Algerian port
13 High school event
15 Blunder
16 Eccentric one
17 Composer Copland
19 Valenzuela
21 "The Greek's" concern
23 Kite
25 Chunk
26 ____ avec nous (God with us)
27 Short road?
28 It's read or red
30 Don or Edie Adams' sign
32 Homophone of earn
34 Part of USNA
36 Consume
37 Grandstander
39 Current
40 Ample, to Byron
41 Smirk
42 Stimulation
44 Silky
46 Rare goose
47 Oceania division
49 Architect Saarinen
51 Iowa tribesman
54 Shebat follower
55 "Ain't ____ Sweet"
57 Dislodge
61 Culminating
64 Chaste
66 Greek architectural style
67 Musteline mammal
68 Box-elder genus
70 Author of the U-Quote
72 Like 70 across
74 Vowel for Plato
75 Hindu exercises
76 Recent: Comb. form
77 Red-cased cheese
79 Ingrid Bergman film: 1956
83 Silver salmon
86 Import

88 Quiet
92 One concern of a wine taster
93 Book size
94 Duo after em
96 Like a tear
97 Singer Tillis
98 Sans ____ (Doric)
99 Trick
101 Begin's predecessor
102 Source of the U-Quote:
    "Portrait of the Artist as a
    Prematurely____"
104 ____-de-sac
106 Beatles movie
108 Knicks' rivals
109 Gaunt
110 Stoicism founder
111 Grooming article, such as
    soap or lotion
113 Crest
115 Siouan
117 Indian garments
118 Thailand's neighbor
119 "Industry" is its motto
120 Boo's brother
121 He fled from Sodom
122 **Middle of the U-Quote**
123 Suffix for lime

DOWN

1 City near Cologne
2 Artemis' friend
3 Hockey player Federko
4 **Start of the U-Quote**
5 Pedro's gold
6 La Guardia was one
7 **End of the U-Quote**
8 Fashionable resorts
9 Altar for a Roman priestess
10 Tasty tidbit
11 Perturbed
14 Unresolved
15 Il Duce's first name
18 Famous Mother
19 Frenzy
20 Actor Bruce
22 Diplomat Silas ____ (1737–89)

24 Turpentine source
25 Tee-hee cousin
28 Belli or Bailey
29 Lacoste of court fame
31 Lukewarm
33 Some merinos
35 An early November duty
38 Plant used in wreaths
41 Sundial style
43 Groucho's "tattooed lady"
45 Speech defect
48 Golfer Lopez, to her friends
50 Side check
51 Bard
52 Kind of sax
53 Give as an example
56 Rye disease
58 ____ even keel
59 Workbench addition
60 Kind of chamber
62 Heavenly streaker
63 Saharan
65 Mystery writer's award
69 Bombay VIP
71 Facilitates
73 It's opposite Philadelphia
78 Jan van der ____ (1632–75)
80 Again
81 Munich's river
82 Former continent?
83 Lombardy lake
84 Riley's friend Digger
85 Place-kicker's aide
87 Celebrant's vestment
89 Filaments
90 Oneness
91 Optician's concern
95 Non-dairy spread
98 Summer shoe
100 Elijah's successor
103 Post
105 Game of chance
107 Tartan
110 Piquancy
112 Celtic language
114 Moo ____ gai pan
116 Dullard

U-QUOTE by John M. Samson

In this puzzle the quotation moves down the length of the diagram, goes across for a bit, and then proceeds all the way up again.

ACROSS

1 Suffix with cloth or front
4 In ____ (beset by problems)
6 Author of the Boxquote
8 Glacial remnant
9 Biographer Winslow
11 **Start of the Boxquote**
14 Source of the Blue Nile
15 Turns
17 Paddock newcomers
18 Soccer great
19 Harp: Ital.
21 Stopover place
22 Bo had them in "10"
24 System of exercises
26 Kind of colony
27 Mix
28 Provides
31 Societal majority
33 Done in
34 Zeta follower
36 Zeno's city
37 Pays attention to
38 Kind of reaction
39 Biblical patriarch
40 P.I.
41 Betty Smith's "____ Grows in Brooklyn"
42 Contentious
44 Prophesied
46 Big
47 Ancient Greek colony
48 Insect nests
49 Barely get by
51 Said further
52 Egyptian king
54 Alea ____ (Cicero's calculated risk)
55 Fugard's "A Lesson from ____"
56 Chapel famous for its frescoes
58 Dramatic conflicts
59 **Boxquote: Part III**
61 Numerical prefix
62 Called
63 Musical intervals
65 Seductive woman
66 European river

DOWN

1 Hadji's religion
2 Gastronomes
3 Caviar source
4 Main artery
5 Ran in the Hambletonian
6 By all ____ (certainly)
7 Isle in a palindrome
8 "And never the twain ____ meet": Kipling
10 A Philippine people
11 **End of the Boxquote**
12 Cone or pyramid
13 **Boxquote: Part II**
14 Complete
16 Masters' "____ River Anthology"
17 Peter or Jane
18 Iron
20 Part of U.S.D.A.
21 Source of the Boxquote: "Le ____ Malgré Lui"
22 Part of an ice skate
23 Employee's concern
25 Glandular
26 Heaped
27 Extorts
29 Partner of square
30 Pore on a leaf
31 Shea player
32 Area over a parrot's beak
33 Tremble
35 Enzyme
38 Mea ____
39 Puzzlers' favorite slaves
41 Assistants
42 Present geological period
43 Mineral deposits
45 Force; power
46 Breakfast cereals
50 Reviewers
51 Not silently
53 Stevie Wonder's "____ She Lovely?": 1976
55 "____ of God," B'way play
57 Edible root
58 Madison Av. group
60 Chalet features
64 Sesame

BOXQUOTE by George P. Sphicas

This quotation moves across, down, backward and then up on the left to form a rectangle. The message, by the way, sounds like a reaction to certain modern poetry.

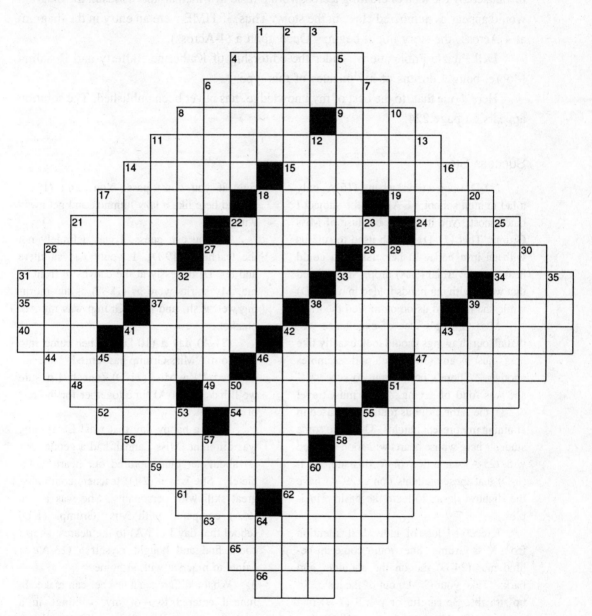

Early in my career as a constructor, Mrs. Farrar introduced me to the Story Crossword. As one who had already published a few short stories in magazines, I was fascinated by the idea of creating a crossword puzzle in which all the words in the diagram would appear as numbered clues in the story. Thus, if TIME were an entry in the diagram at 4 Across, the story might begin: "Once upon a (4-Across). . ."

Dell Puzzle Publications, under the editorship of Katherine Rafferty and Rosalind Moore, bought dozens of my puzzles of this type.

Here's one that, to the best of my knowledge, has never been published. The solution appears on page 224.

Success Story

(31-D) upon a time, when I (16-A) only a lad in high school, (1-A) was the subject I hated most. And it was all because of Miss Grump. That (11-D) grouch used to rule us with an iron hand. In her class you could hear the proverbial (9-A) drop. She insisted that we sit with our hands folded in our (5-D) while she lectured us on outmoded theories.

Miss Grump's idea of excellence was that all our drawings should look exactly like hers—just as any (30-A) in a pod resembles another. "There's no shortcut to success," she was fond of saying. "You must travel (12-D) the same arduous routes that I used in attaining my present heights. There are some students here whose hearts will soon be filled with (25-A) when they (4-A) this subject. It (8-D) that these students don't (29-A) have the slightest desire to learn the basic principles."

I received lots of individual attention from Miss Grump. She would come up behind me, (24-D) me on the shoulder and bark: "Take your (27-D) out of the aisle. Sit up straight. Be careful or you'll (7-D) that bottle of (35-A) paint. It will (17-D) you

right if you don't pass. You can't (15-A) around here like a lazy lummox and get away with it."

As you can guess, I was definitely not the teacher's (19-D). I would just sit there and (14-D) listlessly at the canvas in front of me. My spirits were as (18-A) as the morning wet wash, and Miss Grump was my wet blanket.

(31-A) day a (10-D) teacher came into the room. "Miss Grump has retired," she announced. "I'm Miss (21-D) Zannah. I'm sure we'll have a (34-A) time together for the rest of this term."

What a happy day that was! Everything was different. Miss Zannah had a gentle (33-D) about her that captured our hearts completely. She was a (2-D) teacher, combining great skill with personality. She was a real (6-A) compared with Miss Grump. (1-D) school that day I (13-A) to the nearest shop I could find and bought myself a (23-A) of paints to practice with at home.

What a difference a teacher can make! In June I entered two of my paintings in a contest sponsored by the city fathers. Later they announced that they could not decide which of the many entries was (20-A). They declared a (3-D) for the (32-A) prize. You could have knocked me (11-A) with a feather when I discovered that both winners were mine!

My (26-A) is (29-D) except for one slight addition. Today I (28-D) a pretty penny painting pictures. In fact, I am considered one of the (22-D) top artists in the country. Oh, that Miss Grump could (8-A) me now!

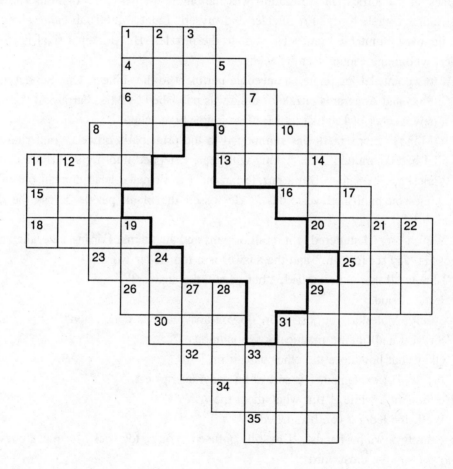

Puns and Anagrams puzzles have been published in the *Times* for more than forty years. Their history is delightfully recounted by Mrs. Farrar in my book *Across and Down*.

These nonsensical crosswords are not only hard to solve but are very difficult to create. Aside from the fact that every word must be clued via some sort of wordplay or an anagram, the restrictions on the constructor are great. For example, the maximum word count is seventy-two—whereas the average 15 × 15 puzzle contains seventy-six or more entries.

Back in the forties, Jack Luzzatto was the chief "perpetrator" of Puns and Anagrams, along with J. Kelly, Ed Buckler and myself. Later, Mel Taub came along and added his own inimitable brand of humor to the puzzles. His principal rival is still Ed Buckler, whom age cannot seem to wither.

At this point, let me relate an anecdote pertinent to the subject. One Sunday in the forties a Puns and Anagrams puzzle of mine was published by Mrs. Farrar. At that time, I was a new teacher of English in a Harlem junior high school.

On Monday morning, I was summoned to the principal's office. Wondering what "crime" I had committed, and shaking with fear, I stepped into my superior's den.

"Maleska," he said, "I'm a puzzle fan but I can't make head nor tail out of that damn thing you published yesterday." He tossed the blank puzzle across the desk. "Explain it!"

"Well, s-sir," I stuttered, "it's full of puns and anagrams. For instance, the clue to 1 Across is 'Jay set for fun?' and the answer is a four-letter word."

"I know all that," he replied, "but what's the answer?"

"Jest," I said.

"Surely, Maleska, you jest. How do you arrive at that conclusion?"

"Sir, jest and fun are practically synonymous."

"Okay, but how does the other part fit in?"

"Jay set," I explained, "is sort of an anagram for jest."

He thought a while. "But what about the A-Y?"

"Well, the letter *J* can be spelled J-A-Y."

He threw down his hands. "I'm still confused. You're too tricky for me. I guess I'll stick to the straight crosswords."

That conversation taught me a lesson. My principal was a very bright man who had a marvelous sense of humor. But like many other intelligent solvers, he never could catch on to the wordplay that permeates Puns and Anagrams.

At any rate, here's a beauty by Mel Taub. I am reprinting it with the permission of the *Times*. The solution awaits you on page 224.

PUNS AND ANAGRAMS by Mel Taub

ACROSS

1 Does tar seem to belong here?
8 Drinking, smoking and de others
15 Inmate finished with pardon?
16 How is a peer to manage?
17 Land with no radar
18 Guard, e.g., at 9:50 A.M.
19 He's a kind of tenant
20 T' perform diplomatically
22 Where Gable came in
23 Creditor's heart
25 Letters on ship
27 But B extinguished
28 Surest color
30 Ishmael has gone the distance
33 Midway at Coney
34 'T aint apple
35 Gets together to trade fees
37 The undoing of a venal girl
39 Drinking place with metal Indian décor
42 9A is vacant
46 Kind o'space
47 Former morning test
48 Broadway's Blossom Lee? Yes!
49 'ad 'addock
51 Raise 51 ft.
53 Seasoning for Emerson?
54 Features of skirts in sale
57 T' go t'seed
59 Kind of lard
60 Maid, 50, is lost
62 Stone found at depot, i.e.
64 Whom to treat as goddess
65 Reactions to Thai raids?
66 Whom one meets in feminist circles
67 They saw cords in bed

DOWN

1 Avalanche gave 'em a scare: SI.
2 O, Ned put the sound higher
3 Up on a new side
4 Color finish
5 Address to Mr. Sahl
6 Parent gets carried away
7 Get to Archie? Not I!
8 Old money, in short
9 Story from Cypriotes
10 Caesar's word of envy, i.e.
11 Girl for Arnie
12 Home of Alec, Tom, Enid, et al.

13 For men, a tie fabric
14 They act with sense at times
21 It let Mimi know how long she had
24 Most artless rulers
26 'T aint active
29 What do 'e do hat Belmont?
31 Kind of sure
32 He's a bird, that is to say
35 Wild flare
36 Miss Egan's first name
38 Plague at 5 E. 10
39 Ahab's A.M. stopover
40 He is alert to the facts
41 He is treat to watch

43 Load Mae with ice cream
44 To him, things that are, e.g., aren't
45 Like some eels? Yes!
48 Pay a visit and score points
50 Alien with Chou
52 Worries that Foster has nothing going
55 To make money, get me out of agreement
56 Eye ____ (socket)
58 Riot beginner
61 Small party
63 Nabokov book that's half daring

Cryptic Crosswords represent the British answer to Arthur Wynne's Word Cross and the subsequent overwhelming popularity of American crossword puzzles. Of course, our linguistic cousins across the Atlantic weren't about to kowtow to the inhabitants of their former colonies and copy their new word game slavishly. Instead, led by Edward Powys Mather (who called himself Torquemada), they invented their own witty and intricate variation of the Wynne winner.

A cryptic puzzle usually has fifteen boxes across and fifteen down. Black squares are numerous, but are diagonally symmetrical. The average puzzle contains only twenty-eight entries as opposed to about seventy-six in an American crossword of the same size. Cryptics seldom contain esoteric words, which I call "crosswordese." You will never find an *anoa* or an *esne* in a British puzzle. However, the disadvantage is that many letters are unkeyed. For example, a letter in a horizontal word is not always crossed by a vertical word.

When my first wife and I traveled to London in 1971, we became hooked on cryptics. One rainy day we stayed in the hotel and bought every British newspaper we could lay our hands on. We liked the challenge of wordplay in the clues, but we became frustrated by English codes for certain letters. Also, we were stumped by references to rugby, cricket and small towns in Great Britain. Finally, there were no explanations to the solutions.

Recognizing that cryptics were somewhat similar to Puns and Anagrams puzzles, I resolved to Americanize the English invention. In 1980 I persuaded Simon and Schuster to publish a book of forty-five cryptic puzzles that contained no Britishisms and provided solvers with explanations of the clues alongside the solutions at the back of the book.

Gradually, the idea caught on in America. By 1988, six books in the series had already been published and demands for Series 7 were pouring in from various parts of the United States and Canada.

Here is an example of an American cryptic. I wish there were room in this book for lengthy explanations of such tricks as *reversals, two meanings, charades, contained* or *hidden words, enclosures,* etc., but you'll find anagrams and puns to get you started even if you have never attempted to solve a cryptic. Incidentally, the numbers in parentheses after the clues indicate the number of letters in the item to be solved. If the numbers are 3-4, you are asked to write a seven-letter hyphenated word. And 7,8 means that the very long entry is split into two parts—a seven-letter word followed by one containing eight letters.

The solution and the explanations appear on page 224.

CRYPTIC CROSSWORD by Fred R. Homburger

ACROSS

1 Excellent selection! (6)
4 Editor who performs on Moscow stage (8)
10 Formerly singular (3-4)
11 Listing of a record following awkward act (7)
12 Quality-control stamp affixed at the bedding factory? (7,8)
13 Put a penny in trust, not so long ago (8)
15 Leading to little street named after an evergreen (5)
18 Try following this river; it might result in trade (5)
19 Part of Pacific Ocean has a nice location (5,3)
22 Should one take British financial backer as a bedfellow? (8,7)
24 Welcoming action in bad weather (7)
25 This letter describes a handgun by its sound (7)
26 Consign in the matter of the French door (8)
27 Gets stuck in cubicles (6)

DOWN

1 Beats hundred tennis players (8)
2 The end of some games (5)
3 Soup ingredient for a cowardly, stocky person? (7,8)
5 Disturb Southern peace and abscond (6)
6 What is needed to pay the check in a fancy restaurant? (5,6,4)
7 Broadcasts that blue jeans fell into river (9)
8 To feast endlessly would be splendid (6)
9 The little salesman of flooring material uncovers a snake (7)
14 Criminal is pleasant and sympathetic (9)
16 Golfer approaching the green is cheerful (7)
17 Mailmen on warships? (8)
20 Is Latin girl a queen of Persia? (6)
21 Reportedly black chess figure? (6)
23 City Renata lives in to some extent (5)

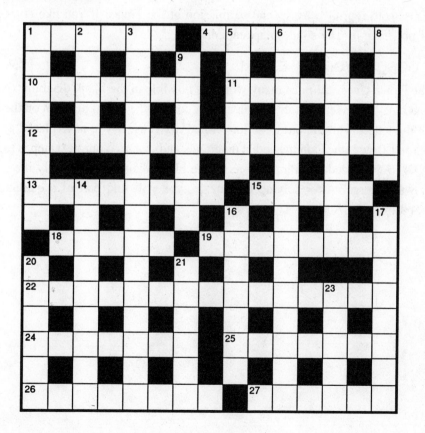

The Cryptocrossword is another of my inventions prompted by a measure of necessity. Every month I receive letters from Sunday *Times* fans asking me to publish a cryptogram. The answer is that there is no room.

However, several years ago it occurred to me that a coded message could be ensconced in a crossword puzzle. I decided that the message should be a familiar quotation or motto.

My first attempt, in which I gave the clues for all the words in the puzzle, proved to be too simple. Then I tried omitting definitions for the horizontal words but including them for the vertical ones. Again, my test solvers said: "It's a cinch! Once we latch on to a few of the Downs, we can decode the puzzle in two shakes of a lamb's tail!"

Finally, I hit upon the right track! The Down words would all be esoteric except for one—or maybe two. Some solvers would have to use reference books to break the code.

And so I summoned up the nerve to publish my first Cryptocrossword. It was not exactly a hit, but it wasn't a flop either. Like my Stepquote, it generated demands from many fans to continue, and it caused others to pronounce it "too hard."

Oh well! Nobody can please all the people all the time. In any case, here's a Cryptocrossword reprinted by special permission of the *Times*. If you like cryptograms, try it. If not, skip it! The solution appears on page 224.

CRYPTOCROSSWORD By E. T. M.

Using the Down clues, fill in as many words as possible in the blank diagram. (Note that no Across clues are given.) After getting a start, consult the coded diagram on the left and compare the letters with the ones you have filled in. Thus, if you have placed a π in the first box for 1 Down, the Q in the coded diagram stands for π. Your next step is to convert all the Q's in the coded diagram into πs in the blank diagram. Gradually the complete solution will emerge. After solving the puzzle, you will find part of a quotation from Horace at 14 and 19 Across.

DOWN

1 Al-____, part of the Syrian Desert
2 King of Sparta: c. 1032 B.C.
3 Today, to Terence
4 Basso Berberian
5 King Lear's interjections: act IV, scene 6
6 Pronunciation mark
7 Paraguayan boundary river
8 Actress Gibbs of "The Jeffersons"
9 Hungarian hero who died in A.D. 907
10 Solid: Comb. form
17 Triangular wooden frame
20 Author Hyman
22 "____ Lady," T. N. Page short story
24 Ship's discarded goods, attached to a buoy
25 Industrial city in Poland
26 Product for use in bleaching and aging flour
27 Old Egyptian game resembling backgammon
29 Group living in Sonora
30 Coating for pills
31 River or canal in Ontario
34 Einstein's equivalent of energy
37 Old wooden pail or tub
39 Chu ____, Chinese leader who helped form the Red Army

Solution grid

1 Q	2 P	3 Q	4 P	5 L	■	6 H	7 P	8 H	9 P	10 L
11 P	V	C	Z	P	■	12 P	N	P	Z	S
13 H	F	X	P	L	■	14 T	P	Z	N	J
15 P	L	F	■	16 P	17 P	Z	■	18 G	P	Z
19 X	F	J	20 H	■	21 N	C	22 H	P	X	J
■	■	23 P	24 G	C	K	J	■	■	■	
25 Z	26 P	27 L	T	P	G	■	28 Q	29 C	30 L	31 S
32 P	V	J	■	33 V	J	34 H	■	35 N	P	Z
36 X	J	K	37 L	J	■	38 P	39 S	P	G	J
40 C	K	F	C	K	■	41 L	J	S	C	K
42 H	J	S	J	X	■	43 L	Q	P	G	S

Empty grid

1	2	3	4	5	■	6	7	8	9	10
11					■	12				
13					■	14				
15			■	16	17		■	18		
19			20	■	21		22			
■	■	23	24				■	■	■	
25	26	27				■	28	29	30	31
32			■	33		34	■	35		
36			37		■	38	39			
40					■	41				
42					■	43				

Wordsmiths' Favorite Word Games

While the manuscript for this book was being written, it occurred to me that readers might be interested in learning what word games are the favorites of people known to have a deep interest in our language. And so I took a sampling of such personages as puzzle constructors, editors, lexicographers, poets, novelists, publishers and columnists.

Starting with those who create or edit crossword puzzles, here are the responses.

Puzzler J. SAMUEL SMART chose the game that my wife and I called *Mishmash*. (See page 25.) His reply reads as follows:

"My favorite word game is The Word Game, as described by H. Allen Smith in one of his early books, probably *Life in a Putty Knife Factory*.

"I expect you are familiar with the game but here is a brief description, just to be safe. The game is played on a 5 × 5 grid of squares. The players take turns calling out letters, each letter to be entered in a square with the object of forming words horizontally and vertically. The last letter is "free." Five-letter words count 10 points; four-letter words, 4 points; and three-letter words, 3 points. Each letter can be counted only once horizontally and once vertically; that is, BARED counts only as BARED, not BARED + BARE + BAR + ARE + RED. Almost any number of people can play, but groups of three, four, or six make for the best games.

"I like the game particularly for its simplicity; pencil and paper are all that is required to get started. Beyond that, it poses interesting questions of strategy. Everyone starts with a high-score solution in mind, but since one individual does not have much control over the entries, a premium is put on flexibility in changing and adapting the game plan. An alternative approach, which is apt to make a user a pariah, is to call only 'problem' letters (*Q, Z, J,* etc.) with the intent of ruining opponents' scores while building up a modest total of one's own."

Constructor STANLEY GLASS agrees with Mr. Smart.

DR. CHARLES DEBER chose Ghost. He added the following:

"For crossword fans, I made up a game: the player is given nine letters, and must arrange them in a 3 × 3 square so that they spell out six words, three across, three down. This can be played competitively, with the winner the first to complete a square. Example: You are given A A B C E G I L P. Possible answer:

C	A	B
A	L	E
P	I	G

JOEL D. LAFARGUE replies that his favorites are puzzles with time limits such as Kriss Kross and Solicross, which appear in Dell crossword puzzle magazines.

BERNICE GORDON's favorite is Categories, and MARY VIRGINIA ORNA has picked what I call Words Within a Word. In that choice she is joined by TRUDE MICHEL JAFFE, editor of daily crosswords for the *Los Angeles Times* Syndicate.

Fictionary was selected by Running Press editor MEL ROSEN. It was also chosen by KENNETH HAXTON, GAYLE DEAN, RICHARD SILVESTRI and NANCY JOLINE. However, Ms. Joline added the following:

"While I enjoy all of the above, they don't produce the high I get from constructing crossword puzzles. I find working on a puzzle such exhilarating mental exercise that I sometimes feel as if my brain cells were tiny gymnasts leaping and cavorting in my head. At other times they are diligent little workers who come up with solutions for me in the middle of the night, or while I'm thinking about something else. Finding just the right word for the right spot is a great feeling."

DOROTHEA SHIPP, who was born in England, naturally prefers cryptic puzzles, and she likes to compete with the contestants on television's "Wheel of Fortune."

DR. ERNST THEIMER's favorite is Fictionary, but he also has something interesting to say about another game.

"We had a variation on Twenty Questions, played mainly when en route some-where. But this well-known game as we played it was hardly the routine variety, and no one ever got close to the answer in less than 100 questions. Two posers I still remember were 'The distance Mount Everest lacks from being 30,000 feet high' and 'The contents of the cubic meter of space 20 meters to the left of the right headlight.' Since we were moving along, this naturally kept changing."

DOUGLAS HELLER, who edits puzzles for Penny Press, prefers a game called Initials. Here's how he explains it:

"On the left margin of a sheet of paper I write the alphabet in a single vertical column. I then locate any sentence of at least 26 letters and begin writing it immediately to the right of the alphabet, one letter per line, again in a vertical column. This creates a set of 26 two-letter initials. When play begins, each person tries to think of the name of a famous person to match each set of initials. Top score: 26."

Mr. Heller also likes a variation of a game described earlier in this book. He calls it License Plate Phrases.

"This is a travel game. On long trips on highways, one sees a great variety of license plates. Most contain some letters, usually two or three. Players spot a license plate and read aloud the letters on that plate. Players then try to think of any legitimate phrase, title, name, etc., which those initial letters match. For example, the license plate 294 MMD would be presented without its numbers as MMD; this might suggest 'Make My Day.' Then you look for another license plate, say RWE 338, which might lead to 'Ralph Waldo Emerson.' If players agree that no suitable entry can be found for a plate, forget it and locate another one."

NANCY ATKINSON's choice is Botticelli, and JEANETTE BRILL's preference is Hang the Man. Interestingly enough, PETER SNOW has selected computer programming as his favorite "word game."

FRED HOMBURGER, an expert constructor of cryptic puzzles, enjoys Scrabble "because it tests one's knowledge of uncommon words and one's ability to visualize unusual combinations of letters and words."

Scrabble is also the choice of constructor JUNE BOGGS. She has included some delightful comments about her family's interest in the game.

"When my brother first returned from Viet Nam, we spent night after night playing Scrabble, often until dawn at which time I stayed up to make breakfasts, pack school lunches, etc., while he had the luxury of going to sleep. It was a questionable luxury, however, because he usually dreamed of gigantic, floating lettered tiles. Despite his 'nightmares,' we always went back for more with the fiendish desire of outdoing each other with seven-letter bonus words.

"Then there was my father who had the audacity to turn some of his tiles over and use them as blanks. It would escape our attention until the end of the game when we discovered five or six blanks on the board instead of the usual two.

"Grandmother, who played well into her nineties, must not go unmentioned. She couldn't wait until the dishes were done to get to a hot game of Scrabble."

ARNOLD MOSS, the famous actor-director who constructs crossword puzzles as a hobby, likes License Plates.

Cryptics constructor WILLIAM COBURN is also a License Plates devotee, and he has several other preferences. Here's what he has to say:

"Driving in traffic we play License Plates—local tags all have three letters and three digits. The idea is to use the three letters in a word consecutively; failing that, spaced out; failing that, in any order. Examples: NGT—'strength'; VHF—'vouchsafe'; JNJ—'jejune'; the idea is to do it in the fewest number of letters. During WW II, shipping from California to India, with one stop in Tasmania, six weeks en route, we played many word games, made puzzles for each other. Anagrams was one; you'd give the guys something like COAL PIPES; imagine the hilarity when that turned out to be EPISCOPAL *and* PEPSI-COLA. Some real stumpers were ROAST MULES, SOHO AND RICE, GORY TUNES, ON THE CLIPS.

"Also played Hangman—some were hung by JUKEBOX, CRAZYQUILT, and such like. The solving strategy was like "Wheel of Fortune"—TSRNHL, but always preceded by the vowels. CRWTH fooled no one. [And] Acronyms—take the name of a famous person (short names are best!) and try to make something appropriate of the letters in it. I can recall no really good examples from yesteryear, but IACOCCA recently came up: I Am Chairman of Chrysler Corporation of America."

Another License Plates aficionado is VAUGHAN KEITH. He has invented several variations of the game and enjoys creating long words. For example, he once converted TNM into TRANSMIGRATION.

WILL SHORTZ, a senior editor at *GAMES,* has invented his own variation of Word Association, which he calls Associations. (In this case, I will not use quotation marks.)

Associations is a word game for any number of players (four to fifteen is best). One more person is needed as moderator. The game is played in two parts. Part 1 is a noncompetitive exercise of forming a chain of word associations. The moderator gives a starting word (any one will do), and the first player calls out a word associated with it. Then the next player calls out a word associated with the first player's word (preferably not related to the one before it). Then the third player calls out a word associated with the second player's word, and so on, around the circle, continuing for fifty or more words. The moderator makes a list of all the words in the chain.

A sample chain might begin LOVE, TENNIS, COURT, SUPREME, DIANA ROSS, etc. Answers may be words of any variety. The associations should be ones that are understood by all players. Punning is permissible.

In Part 2 of the game, the chain is reversed, and players try to recall the list of words in reverse order. (Players may or may not be told about this aspect of the game before they begin Part 1.) For example, if the end of the chain were CARROT, RABBIT, VOLKSWAGEN, and BUG, the moderator would say "stop," give the word BUG, and ask the next player what word preceded it. Then the following player would be asked to give the word preceding *it*. And so on.

If a player can't remember the next preceding word, he or she receives a point, and the following player tries to give the word. If no player in the group can remember a particular word, the moderator gives the answer and the game continues.

The player with the fewest points at the end of the game wins.

JOHN KEENAN, editorial coordinator for *GAMES*, has responded as follows:

"I do enjoy the 'Gene Traub–like' word games that are featured in the Pencilwise section of *GAMES* magazine. These puzzles feature a clue word such as *pen* or *van* and all the answers contain this clue word (i.e., Pennsylvania, vanilla, etc.)."

MAURA JACOBSON, who creates the big puzzles for *New York,* submits a game that she has enjoyed for many years. Since she cannot remember the name, I'll call it Alphabetics.

Object: to make two-word phrases, names or places. First words must all begin with the same letter. Second words must begin with all the letters of the alphabet.

Preparation: write letters of the alphabet down the middle of a paper.

Number of Players: two or more; the more the better.

Time Limit: about five minutes.

Scoring: One point for each acceptable phrase, name or place. No credit if another player has the same pair. Highest score wins.

EXAMPLE USING THE LETTER C:

CHARGE	ACCOUNT	CASEY	JONES	COMMON	STOCK
CAROL	BURNETT	CALVIN	KLEIN	COFFEE	TABLE
CHINESE	CHECKERS	CRASH	LANDING	COLUMBIA	UNIVERSITY
CHRISTIAN	DIOR	COPPER	MINE	CYRUS	VANCE
CHANCE	ENCOUNTER	CARDINAL	NUMBER	CRIMEAN	WAR
CHEESE	FONDUE	CINCINNATI	OHIO	CHEST	X-RAY
CHORUS	GIRL	CLOSE	QUARTERS	CEILING	ZERO
CONEY	ISLAND	COLORADO	RIVER		

The same word cannot be used twice in the first column.

Puzzlemaker WILLIAM CANINE has sent me the following reply.

"Favorite word game? I would be less than honest were I not to confess that constructing crossword puzzles is now far and away my favorite word game. And constructing *is* a game, even if I only play it against myself. It has the virtues of chess: there is no luck involved. With two players, Scrabble is a grand game, of course, and I like anagrams too, but for me constructing a crossword puzzle is the most fun."

Constructor LOU SABIN is a Scrabble fan. His second choice is Fictionary, which he calls Dictionary.

Like Mr. Canine, puzzler LOU BARON has only one love—creating crosswords. Here's his response.

"From the first moment I met crossword puzzles I was hooked. Its pheromones drew me like an animal in the rutting season; combined with my love of Bach, Beethoven and Mozart I found the ideal harmonic combo that have more in common than you would think. Is it so fanciful to equate puzzle-sculpting with musical composition? So I enjoy creating puzzles, some of which blossom and intermesh like a toccata and fugue by J.S.B., while others sweat and strain and are duds, stillborns kind of. Considering that Xwords are surely a word game, and further contemplating that I am a hopeless junkie in the lure of their challenge, no other word game ever had a chance. Exploiting the musical analogy once more, I enjoy the theme and variations, the symphonic sonorities, the harmonies and the interweaves which often leave one wondering: Where did the final product come from?"

What's a pheromone? Let me quote *Webster's New World Dictionary:* "Any of various chemical substances secreted externally by certain animals, as ants, moths, etc., which convey information to, and produce specific responses in other individuals of the same species."

Well, I suppose that's what crossword puzzles do for Homo sapiens.

Constructor JACK STEINHARDT is a Hanky-Panky fan, but he calls the game Inky-Stinky. Mr. Steinhardt's contributions are:

luxurious snack — posh nosh
pusillanimous expert — craven maven
procrastinating knave — laggard blackguard
prevailing astronomical instrument — extant sextant

THOMAS MIDDLETON, the dean of Acrostics, enjoys the Galli-Maltby puzzles in *Harper's* and the Cox-Rathvon puzzles in *The Atlantic*. His second choice is Superghost.

Mr. Middleton adds the following:

"My wife and I also enjoy an occasional round of Big Boggle, which is a simple game, but we've made it a little more difficult by limiting ourselves to words of five or more letters, instead of four or more. Finding a word of nine or ten letters on a Big Boggle throw is always a thrill."

Constructor BERT ROSENFIELD's answer will please Mr. Middleton. The wordsmith from Troy, New York, is an acrostics addict.

LOIS SIDWAY could not make up her mind. She likes versions of Hang the Man, as well as Categories and Mike Shenk's Anti-Match Game. Lois formerly belonged to a Connecticut group called the Fairfield County Puzzlers. In that connection, she writes:

"An original (far as I know) little word challenge I presented once was for everyone to try to come up with two six-letter words, the second letter of each being the only vowel in the word. After a few minutes, it was necessary for me to give hints—the first letters of the words—and soon one of the members came up with DIRNDL and WARMTH. (They had to be in the Funk & W's word-finder book. There's also PUTSCH, but it's capitalized and foreign.)"

Actor-constructor WALTER COVELL, who plays the part of Colonel Mustard in the VCR version of the game called Clue, is another advocate of the pastime that I have designated as Mishmash. For some strange reason he calls it Eppizootics.

Mr. Covell's addendum reads as follows:

"A variation of the game is for each player to use two grids at once, entering the letters, as they are called, in either grid. This is especially recommended for crossword-puzzle constructors, since, when they have become increasingly stymied by difficult opponents who spoil their plans by calling useless letters, they will much more appreciate the relative ease with which, in noncompetitive situations, they can weave words, however elusive and cantankerous, in their commercially submitted puzzles."

Puzzler ALFIO MICCI, former first violinist for the New York Philharmonic Orchestra, likes to play Probe and Jotto with his wife, Martha.

Constructor BARRY L. COHEN fondly remembers The Sphinx Page, which was part of a defunct publication called *The 4☆ Puzzler*. One of the features was the uses of *x*'s and *y*'s in place of other letters in verses such as limericks. An example is cited below:

> There was a young athlete from Minn. U.
> Who was xxxyxx of frame and of sinew.
> But he hated to xxxxx;
> His mind became muddy.
> So at Minn. U. he could not continue.
>   (Answer: sturdy/study)

Alan Arbesfeld, who creates regular crosswords as well as puns and anagrams puzzles, likes a commercial game called Perquackey. His description of the game reads:

"The game is played with 13 lettered cubes, and the object is to spell as many words as possible within a fixed time limit (using a sand-timer), with no more than five words containing the same number of letters allowed in a given turn. The cubes are rolled and more points are awarded for words of greater length, with bonus points given for completing all five words of a particular length."

Mr. Arbesfeld also mentions a game that he calls Printer's Deviltry. An example is an offshoot of: "As if protected by armor, Ali stayed uncut through most of his fights."

The solver is told that the hidden word has eight letters. The answer, as most cryptics solvers know, is *moralist* (combining letters from ar*mor Ali* and *st*ayed). But that's too easy! In Printer's Deviltry the sentence would read: "As if protected by a ray, Ed—uncut through most of his fights." The solver is required to supply *armor, Ali stayed* in the place of *a ray.*—Ed uncut.

Mr. Arbesfeld may enjoy such double jeopardy, but I prefer less diabolical combinations requiring only one leap of the brain. For example:

> It's served to some extent on real U.N. china. (LUNCH)
> Patriotic song coming from a giant he-man. (ANTHEM)
> A piece of good earth in short supply. (DEARTH)

Constructor Joy Wouk's choice is Jotto, and Shirley Soloway likes Scrabble and Boggle. Her preference for the latter game is shared by Dr. Robert Wolfe, but he opts for the larger version.

Puzzler Arthur Palmer holds forth for Word Associations.

Dr. Warren Reich has come up with an unusual game that he calls Alphabok. It requires two hundred letters in the "boneyard." A title or phrase of at least twenty letters is laid out vertically. For example, *All's Well That Ends Well* goes down. Now each player must create a ten-letter word going across. The first word might be *adjudicate* and the second *lachrymose,* etc.

My feeling is that Dr. Reich must have many bright friends who have a store of ten-letter words in their brains.

Mᴇʟ Tᴀᴜʙ is probably the world's most versatile puzzler. In almost a twinkling, he can create an acrostic, a cryptic puzzle, a puns and anagrams teaser, or any other crossword worth mentioning. But Mel's response to me was most modest. He states that he once thought he was an expert Scrabble player until he played with some strangers at an Adirondacks resort. They trounced him and he never recovered from the humiliation.

Mel has settled for Jotto as his favorite word game, but he tells an interesting story about his ability in orthography when he was a child. He talks about a fourth-grade spelling bee:

"The field had narrowed to two skinny ten-year-olds, Muriel and myself. The word September was presented to me. Without hesitation I rattled off s-e-p-t-e-m-b-e-r and was declared wrong. Muriel, with a smirk, countered with *capital* S-e-p-t-e-m-b-e-r and walked off with the first and only prize, a 10-cent Scripto pencil with red lead. That I can remember this vividly almost half a century later proves I never got over it. I often wonder what happened to Muriel and whether she still has the pencil."

Mel's sad tale reminds me of one of my own. There were two eighth-grade classes in my grammar school. I won the spelling bee in my class and a girl named Eleanor Boland triumphed in the other section.

We were called before the principal—an aged woman who told us that the winner might go on to represent the school in a national spelling bee at Washington, D.C. She then proceeded to call off such toughies as *precipitous, phlegm, embarrass* and *accommodate*—all of which we spelled correctly.

Finally, with a deep sigh, the principal said, "Eugene, spell Eleanor."

I responded, "Capital E-l-i-n-o-r."

"Wrong!" cried the principal. "Miss Boland?"

My competitor promptly responded: "Capital E-l-e-a-n-o-r" and was declared the winner. Apparently our administrator had never heard of poet-novelist Elinor Wylie—but neither had I.

At any rate, with tears in my eyes, I trudged home and felt that I had been cheated.

Eleanor Boland was eliminated immediately in the city's competition. At the tenth reunion of our class, I happened to sit next to her and I asked her if she remembered our knock-down-and-drag-out contest in the principal's office.

She smiled and said, "Yes. As I recall, I finally beat you!"

"You certainly did," I replied, "but can you tell me the word that tripped me up?"

She shook her head. "No, what was it?"

At that moment, I could have choked Eleanor!

STANLEY B. WHITTEN, a puzzlemaker from Illinois, gets lots of enjoyment from Jotto. Like most others, he assumes that the game is played only with five-letter words. As described earlier in chapter 2, I had played equivalents of Jotto (long before it became commercialized) with four-letter words, and even six- and seven-letter words.

Mr. Whitten points out a human problem that sometimes occurs when playing against a sleepy or obtuse person. As poet Archibald MacLeish once wrote: It's an "appallment."

"The only drawback I've found in the game is the rare occasion when my opponent discounts the coinciding letters and provides me with a wrong answer. This of course throws the whole game off and can prompt one to direct certain five-letter words like DUMMY or STUPE at one's opponent."

Veteran constructor SIDNEY L. ROBBINS says that his present addiction is puns and riddles such as:

" 'You *tire* me out,' said the road to the auto."

"Champagne to our real friends; real pain to our sham friends."

"Where will you find the last man? (In a shoe factory.)"

Mr. Robbins also has this to say about his younger days:

"Word games have long been used on extended auto trips to occupy the minds of restless children. The ages of the youngsters involved are of course a factor to be considered in determining the degree of sophistication involved in any particular word game.

"We all recall the pastime named by some as Geography wherein the leader starts by giving a city, ocean, or locale, let's say, *New York.* The next player uses the last letter, in this case *K,* to start his or her word, such as *Kansas. S* would start the next response, such as *San Francisco,* and so on."

*   *   *

JIM PAGE, whose Sunday *Times* challengers are famous or infamous (depending on the experience of the solver) joins Sidney Robbins in his preference for punny word games. His favorite is a spin-off from the Word Association game described earlier (page 137).

What follows is Mr. Page's description of a word game invented by him and his friends. Note how wordplay is involved. I have never participated in this game, but I think I would enjoy it—especially at a party in which witty people are gathered. I'll omit quotes.

We made up a game called Keep It Going, in which two or more players may participate. Player #1 starts off by coming up with a sentence five words or more in length, let's say, for example, "It sure is hot today." Player #2 selects a word from that sentence to get the theme of the game. Thus, he might respond, "Anyone seen *Blazing Saddles?*" By choosing "blazing," #2 has set the theme (heat), and Player #3 must keep it going by coming up with a response containing a synonym or associated word for "heat." For instance, he might come back with "That really *burns* me up." Successive responses in this sample game might include, "I can't *warm up* to this game"; "Don't be so *stuffy*"; "That's a *sticky* wicket"; and so forth. When the opportunity presents itself, a player may change the theme in the middle of the game. Thus, in this sample game, a player may say, "It's like an *oven* in here" and get the response, "I've got a *heater* in my pocket," setting up the next player's chance to change the theme from "heat" to "weapons," which he does with "You son of a *gun,*" followed by weapons-oriented comments such as, "I feel *pistol*-whipped"; "Remember 'The *Rifle*man' on TV?"; "*Rod* Cameron's my favorite actor"; "the slings and *arrows* of outrageous fortune"; etc.

Here are the rules:

- Opening sentence must be five words or more.
- Two players or more may participate.
- Anyone unable to keep it going gets an *L,* until with five misses (picking up *O, S, E, R*) he is eliminated.
- Responses must be at least two words in length and may include phrases any length, quotes, slangy quips, puns and, of course, made-up sentences.

No theme word may be repeated, and, for the tigers of this world for whom winning is everything, time limits may be imposed. To my mind, the fun of Keep It Going is in the length of each game and the number of groans elicited for awful puns and word-stretches.

SAMPLE GAME

Player #1: Money is the root of all evil.
#2: Makes *cents* to me.
#3: *Penny* for your thoughts.
#4: To *coin* a phrase.
#5: I have a *yen* for a hamburger.
#1: *Mark* my words.
#2: Aw, go *pound* the pavement.
#3: You *lettuce* alone.
#4: That's *corny*.
#5: *Beats* me.
#1: Remember the Giants' Willie Mays (*maize*)?

(*Note:* "Lettuce," as in slang for paper money, sets the stage for a theme switch, which Player #4 takes advantage of.)

WILL WENG, who edited *New York Times* puzzles before me and who is still active in the world of crosswords, makes this surprising statement:

"My favorite game of yesteryear wasn't really a word game but a card game called I Doubt It, in which players could be truthful or untruthful in announcing what cards they were putting on the table, facedown. Successful chicanery was the goal. To me the game was an adventure in flouting convention and a harmless respite from conforming to established codes."

However, I happen to know that Mr. Weng enjoys Fictionary because I've played that game with him on several occasions.

Speaking of editors, my colleague in the preparation of numerous volumes of the *Simon and Schuster Crossword Puzzle Book* is JOHN SAMSON. In response to my inquiry, he had several interesting things to say.

"I would have to say the crossword puzzle is my favorite word game. Since I earn my living solely through crosswords, the choice is a relatively easy (and biased) one. My favorite puzzle is the *New York Times Magazine* crossword. I get a kick out of those fair-but-misleading clues. For example, if the clue were 'Hall of fame,' the answer might be FAWN. A word like IGLOO might be clued 'Northern hemisphere.'

"Another reason I enjoy solving crosswords is because it's a solitary sport. It's like golf in that respect. In golf it's you against the course. In crossword solving it's you against those little blank squares. Both can be performed alone. The word *alone* is significant. I gave up playing all board games, when, after beating my wife at Scrabble for ten consecutive times, she wouldn't talk to me for a week. She claims I tend to gloat after a victory. I personally think she's wrong, but that's rather academic now. That was years ago.

"The killer instinct has left me now. No longer do I enjoy killing innocent pawns and bishops in chess. No longer do I laugh as my neighbor is frantically mortgaging his Monopoly holdings as I'm greedily erecting hotels on Boardwalk and Park Place. No longer do I play these games. My life is more peaceful and less stressful now. When I want to relax, I retreat to a vacant room and play a few games of solitaire and sharpen my pencil for those little blank squares."

The father-daughter combination of ALEX AND VICTORIA BLACK is probably familiar to many Sunday *Times* puzzle fans. Their favorite game is different from all the others in this chapter. I will omit quotation marks in citing their very clever response:

You must be familiar with Tom Swifties, which we gamely offer as our favorite.

A few examples in the manner of dear old Tom:

"I must go to the dermatologist," he said rashly.
"I need new tires," he said baldly.
"The present is perfect," he said tensely.

Tom Swifties require no equipment other than a sharp mind, we say pointedly, and become very competitive, we state winningly, when one player tries to top another's Swifty on the same subject. Like this:

"I'll have soup," she ordered wantonly (looking at Chinese menu).
"Make mine egg drop," he cackled.

Can you imagine having dinner with the Blacks? "You'd have to be on your toes," said Gene outstandingly.

And now, let's turn to the favorite word games of famous people who are not crossword-puzzle constructors or editors.

First and foremost is RICHARD WILBUR, the successor to Robert Penn Warren as

America's poet laureate. Mr. Wilbur's preference is Anagrams, and his description of the game is related in chapter 2. I also happen to know that he and his wife, Charlee, are addicted to the Sunday *Times* crossword puzzle.

Mr. Wilbur's comparison of Anagrams with Scrabble is interesting: "In Anagrams one concentrates on letters and words; in Scrabble there is letter-value and rack-and-board pattern to cope with, and that leads to the spelling of unheard-of words and the compiling of bonus lists. Anagrams, though it can be very exciting and can be brilliantly played, remains an amateur game; Scrabble, it seems to me, is a game conducive to tension, pallor and talk about experts and grand masters. My guess is that a good Anagrams player gets to act upon more of his good ideas than a good Scrabble player does."

I echo Mr. Wilbur's feelings. See my comments about Scrabble in chapter 3.

Our poet laureate goes on to say that he also likes Superghost, cryptics puzzles and puns and anagrams crosswords.

Poet JAMES MERRILL, who won a Pulitzer Prize for his *Divine Comedies* in 1976, has sent a fascinating and unusual reply:

"Anagrams is certainly a leading contender. I'd been playing it with myself for years before sitting down to my first cutthroat session in Key West with John Brinnin, John Ciardi, and Richard Wilbur. Here with my own eyes I saw Ciardi turn PITCHERS into SPHINCTER, with my own ears heard how Leonard Bernstein once made an ORCHESTRA out of ROACHES. Heady stuff for one who until then had merely divined A NICE SCARE in a SCENIC AREA, or the EVER TENSED VIOL in DENISE LEVERTOV. Such freakish relationships among words can arouse a genealogist's passion—and reduce the player to nervous exhaustion. In the long run I've found a couple of hours at the Ouija board more refreshing. It is easy to make your own: take a sheet of heavy paper, inscribe it with the alphabet and the Arabic numerals, use an overturned teacup as pointer. Now you and your partner, no matter how sleepy or how skeptical, are in business. The messages, often highly literate, come from . . . outer space? your own subconscious minds? It hardly matters. Here at last is a game in which the players, relieved of both luck and ingenuity, have only to sit back and reap their rewards."

Author WILLIAM STYRON, who won the Pulitzer Prize for literature in 1967 for *The Confessions of Nat Turner* and who also gave us *Sophie's Choice* in 1979, is a modest man. His answer to my query will surprise and delight you.

"My favorite over the years has been Anagrams. My wife, Rose, is an absolute genius at most word games, especially Scrabble, but in past years I have beaten down my sense of inferiority to play word games with her. She and our friend Leonard Bernstein are about on the same level—which is to say uncannily good—and I have always withdrawn from the fray whenever both of them were involved in a game. However, some years ago when I was still relatively unintimidated and brash enough to play Anagrams with Rose and Lenny I scored a prodigious coup by any standards. The change was this: I converted in one fell swoop THERAPY into PHYLACTERIES. I remember Lenny's consternation and his observation that this was an extremely Jewish ploy for a Presbyterian to execute. However, I'm afraid there was a great deal of dumb luck involved in the maneuver. I never came even remotely close to any such brilliant change again and so, as I say, withdrew more or less permanently from Anagrams, at least in play against world-class opponents like Rose and Lenny.''

Lexicographer DAVID B. GURALNIK, who fathered the outstanding *Webster's New World Dictionary,* presented me with a detailed and delightful reply.

''I do enjoy playing with language, having long been addicted to punning, although I've learned over the years to exercise restraint in the company of those who don't share my predilection for that art.* I also like to write occasional light verse, including limericks, bawdy or sanitized, and usually also involving puns. And, as I believe I've told you, I have in recent years rediscovered the crossword puzzle, especially the newer variety involving, again, puns, as well as rebuses, themes, and the like, and I enjoy matching wits, with the constructors. I've gotten pretty good at solving and can now generally complete the Sunday *Times* puzzle in from 30 to 40 minutes.

''But I don't actually get any pleasure from playing formalized word games, especially the anagrammatic ones, like Scrabble, that merely involve the mechanical manipulation of letters to form words, and so I avoid them. At small parties, with the right people, charades can be a lot of fun, as can be an exchange of creative punning, such as this game, first introduced to me at a dictionary-society dinner some years ago. Here's the premise: If lawyers are disbarred and priests unfrocked, what words would you apply to

*''Spontaneity is, of course, the hallmark of a good pun. One of my better efforts occurred on a trip to Scandinavia a number of years back. We were on an obligatory tour of a palace in Copenhagen and in a room filled with portraits of past monarchs. Our guide was explaining one picture of four vacuous youths, each the son of King Olaf the Somethingth, and all of whom had later become rulers of one Scandinavian country or another. Bored, I was staring up at the ceiling, that sported a large, irregular stain. 'What do you find so interesting up there?' asked one of my travel companions. 'I guess the plumbing isn't so great in these palaces,' I replied, adding 'but a royal flush beats four kings any time.' In the hilarity of the moment, neither of us paused to consider that you can't have four kings and a royal flush in the same round of poker.''

practitioners of other occupations who have lost their positions? Sample answers: Song writers are decomposed; tavern owners are disjointed; hookers are delayed (or unscrewed?); etymologists are debased (or uprooted); and puzzlers are dissolved. The possibilities are endless.''

With regard to Mr. Guralnik's last sentence, I assume that he has never allowed wild cards to intrude in his poker games.

Mr. Guralnik's refreshing word game in his second paragraph caused me to brush off my brain cells and try for some new ones. Here are my additions:

> Colonists are unsettled.
> Carpenters are deplaned.
> The B.P.O.E. is dismembered.
> Rock stars are disconcerted.

WILLARD R. ESPY, who has written *An Almanac of Words at Play* and other publications dealing with joyful aspects of our language, has contributed two of his own creations along with an introduction. Since I have made a few minor changes, quotation marks will not be used. He says:

Friends describe me as better at causing problems than at solving them. This is a canard overall, but true enough when it comes to word puzzles. My favorite puzzles are those I arrange myself: I know the answers.

Since my head jingles more than it thinks, it is also true that my puzzles are usually in rhyme. They involve any of four different kinds of wordplay; acrostics; anagrams; word pyramids; or doublets. Examples of two of these genres follow, each preceded by an explanation of how the game is played.

ESPYGRAM

Anagram verses—I call mine ESPYgrams—must date back at least fifty years; it is my memory that Phyllis Fraser was writing them for the *Saturday Review* at the time of the Second World War, and perhaps earlier. They are rhymes in which certain words, each an anagram of the rest, are omitted, and the reader is challenged to recreate them by examining the context and, in certain cases, words with which they rhyme. In the following example, there is no rhyme to help. You will doubtless assume from the first two lines that the speaker has expressed a desire to sire an offspring, and that the mother-to-be has taken kindly to the suggestion. The third and fourth lines indicate a certain disillusionment on her part. Perhaps the likely past tense of the first two missing words, indicating that they may have ended in -ed, will help. ''Wanted,'' for instance, would seem to make sense; unfortunately, it is too short to fill the blanks. "Desired" fits, but the only anagram for it that occurs to me offhand is "resided," and that would be of no use in any of the three remaining blanks. I might say, though, that few of my friends take more than three or four minutes to solve the puzzle.

When I __ __ __ __ __ __ __ to be a father,

You __ __ __ __ __ __ __ my willingness to bother.

Now you __ __ __ __ __ __ __ ; you never knew

I'd leave the __ __ __ __ __ __ __ to you.

WORD PYRAMID

A word pyramid begins with a one-letter word, adds a letter to make a new word, and continues to increase the word length a letter at a time, rearranging the order of the letters each time as needed to turn them into a word. Thus:

O

T O

T O P

P O S T

P O E T S

T O P E R S

R I P O S T E

S P O R T I E R

P O S T E R I O R

The procedure may be reversed, starting with a long word and reducing it step by step to a single letter.

ESPYramids Up and ESPYramids Down are verses involving such pyramids. Dashes substitute for the letters. You need only fill in the word. This ESPYramid Up is as sensible as most of them:

—worm once in __ __ apple grew;

An old __ __ __ bit the worm in two

(A __ __ __ __ and naughty thing to do).

The two halves __ __ __ __ __ him in a suit.

They made __ __ __ __ __ __ he restitute

Their former state inside the fruit.

Their lot could not __ __ __ __ __ __ __ be,

Which __ __ __ __ __ __ __ them, as it would me.

The solutions to the preceding two puzzles appear on page 224.

Incidentally, it should be noted that the first of the two originally appeared in a book called ESPYgrams and the other was published in Mr. Espy's *Word Puzzles*.

Songwriter-lyricist STEPHEN SONDHEIM has replied: "Thanks for the invitation but I'm no good at prose." However, I happen to know that Mr. Sondheim has created his own brand of cryptic puzzles and is also a fine anagrams player.

Lyricist SAMMY CAHN derives special pleasure from finding innovative, unusual rhymes that fit perfectly with the notes created by one of his many collaborators. Mr. Cahn adds: "My favorite word game is to change the words of all the great songs, for instance, 'You're Getting to Be a Habit with Me.'

"Once or twice would be nice;
Lately now it won't suffice:
She's getting to be a RABBIT with me."

MARY ANN MADDEN, whose wordplay contests are featured in *New York* magazine, states that her favorite word game is called Bartlett's—a variety of Fictionary that my daughter Merryl and I thought we had invented.

One person selects a brief quotation from an author whose name and dates are announced to the group. The first part of the quotation is read to the group and each player then finishes it in the hope that some competitor will be fooled into thinking that the completion was the original one. In such cases, the "fooler" gets 1 point for each vote that he or she has garnered.

Ms. Madden once completed "If music be the food of love. . ." by adding, "count me out." She was rewarded with laughter but no votes.

ROBERT KATZ is the author of many books. His novel *The Cassandra Crossing* was made into a very successful movie. Mr. Katz is also a crossword-puzzle constructor. He writes: "My favorite game is word processing on the computer and dreaming up time-saving macros . . . the incorporation of a whole bunch of keystrokes into one."

BEVERLY SILLS GREENOUGH tells me that her current passion is playing Scrabble in Italian, using only musical themes, composers' names, titles of operas, directors, singers, stage designers, and so on.

Beverly adds: "The participants are generally members of the opera tribe; otherwise it doesn't work.'' That observation leads me to say platitudinously: ''You can say *that* again!''

W‍ILLIAM F. B‍UCKLEY's laconic reply was: ''I'd gladly cooperate except I play no word games. Best of luck.'' Upon reading that message, my son Gary quipped: ''Mr. Buckley plays word games every time he opens his mouth. What a vocabulary!''

Author-screenwriter E‍RNEST L‍EHMAN sent me a fascinating reply re his favorite word game.

''You take words of various lengths, short, medium and long, of different genres such as nouns, pronouns, verbs, adverbs, adjectives, conjunctions and prepositions, and you put these words down one after another in such manner as to make another person, upon reading them, laugh, cry, be moved, question something, or understand something.

''It's called *writing.*''

Three *New York Times* executives have sent me diversified replies. Managing Editor A‍RTHUR G‍ELB, who is a recognized authority on the life and works of Eugene O'Neill, has chosen a variety of Jotto (q.v.) as his favorite word game.

J‍ACK R‍OSENTHAL, who is an editorial page editor and author of many etymological articles, has a surprising answer: ''In truth, my favorite word game is constructing crossword puzzles with puns in them.''

M‍ARJORIE L‍ONGLEY, the dynamic ex-director of public affairs for the *Times,* makes me feel elated because she confesses that she loves to curl up with my puzzle each morning over a cup of coffee. Since her nickname is Midge, she sometimes cringes when she is described as a ''gnat'' in an occasional crossword puzzle.

J‍OSEPH C‍OTTEN has the same passion as Ms. Longley. His day always begins with a cup of coffee and a *Times* crossword puzzle.

F‍RANK S‍INATRA is another star who is addicted to *Times* puzzles. He is proud to announce that he solves them in ink. (My definition of an optimist.) When he takes long flights on his private plane, he makes sure that he has brought along a slew of crosswords.

In conclusion, I might say that word games seem to be loved by millions of Americans, whether famous or anonymous members of the multitudes, from Maine to California. Anagrams, Scrabble, License Plates, Fictionary and crossword puzzles apparently lead the pack—not necessarily in that order.

In connection with the last of that illustrious list, I think that an appropriate ending to this book is to share a poem on crosswords published by Richard Wilbur in the May 1985 issue of *The New Yorker*.

ALL THAT IS
Twilight approaches, with its last brief spot-lit
Galaxies of midges, its first star,
And having put in doubt its bats or swallows,
Enters the eastern suburbs. There the hedged
Air darkens like a fast-reducing broth,
Simmering the shapes of things. And counter to
Those topiary whims, those *carceri,*
That cypress dye which taints the arbor vitae,
Bright squares flash on in staggered patterns, block
By block, some few blacked out by lowered shades.
Meanwhile, through evening traffic and beneath
Checkered façades, a many-lighted bus,
Pausing or turning at the intersections,
Goes intricately home. One passenger
Already folds his paper to the left-
Hand lower corner of the puzzles page,
As elsewhere other hands are doing, whether
At kitchen tables under frazzled light,
In plumped-up sickbed, or the easy chair
Near which a faceted decanter glows.
Above this séance, in the common dark
Between the street-lamps and the jotted sky,
What now takes shape? It is a ghostly grille
Through which, as often, we begin to see
The confluence of the Oka and the Aare.

Is it a vision? Does the eye make out
A flight of ernes, rising from aits or aeries,
Whose shadows track across a harsh terrain
Of esker and arête? At waterside,
Does the shocked eeler lay his lampreys by,

Sighting a Reo driven by an edile?
And does the edile, from his running board,
Step down to meet a ranee? Does she end
By reading to him from the works of Elia?
No, there are no such chance encounters here
As you imagined once, O Lautréamont,
No all-reflecting prism-grain of sand
Nor eyeful such as Markandeya got
When, stumbled into vacancy, he saw
A lambent god reposing on the sea,
Full of the knitted light of all that is.
It is a puzzle which, as puzzles do,
Dreams that there is no puzzle. It is a rite
Of finitude, a picture in whose frame
Roc, oast, and Inca decompose at once
Into the ABCs of every day.
A door is rattled shut, a deadbolt thrown.
Under some clipped euonymus, a mushroom,
Bred of an old and deep mycelium
As hidden as the webwork of the world,
Strews on the shifty night-wind, rising now,
A cast of spores as many as the stars.

RICHARD WILBUR

Answers
and Solutions

FICTIONARY

gabarit—answer 6: an outline on a drawing of an object

hicatee—answer 5: a West Indian freshwater tortoise

ridotto—answer 7: public entertainment consisting of music and dancing

deipnosophist—answer 2: one skilled in the art of table talk

• • •

ataraxia—calmness of the mind and emotions

auscultation—listening

benthos—the bottom of a body of water, especially the ocean

bolometer—instrument for measuring and recording small amounts of radiant energy

bombazine—a twilled cloth of silk and rayon

calendula—the pot marigold

cavetto—a concave molding

demulcent—soothing

euphorbia—spurge

fastigiate—sloping toward a point

fimbriate—having a fringe of hairs, fibers, etc.

gaselier—an early ornamental chandelier

grisaille—a style of painting, especially on glass

hubris—wanton insolence or arrogance

huckaback—a coarse linen or cotton cloth

innervate—to stimulate a nerve or muscle

jacinth—a reddish-orange color

jactation—the act of bragging

koto—a Japanese musical instrument

lovage—plant of the parsley family

lugger—a small vessel

myrmecology—study of ants

nankeen—durable cotton cloth

objurgate—to chide vehemently

picul—a unit of weight used in southeast Asia

pyretic—causing fever

quodlibet—an academic debate

recusant—dissenter or nonconformist

sequacious—dependent, servile

talipot—a fan palm of the East Indies

triturate—pulverize

usquebaugh—whiskey

ustulate—discolored

valgus—knock-kneed

williwaw—sudden, violent cold wind

xanthous—yellow

yamen—residence of a mandarin

yataghan—a Turkish saber with a double-curved blade

zareba—a camping place in the Sudan

zarf—a small, metal holder used in the Levant for a hot coffee cup

FICTIONARY VARIATIONS

Last Lines (prose)

1. "Cabs and omnibuses hurried to and fro, and crowds passed, hastening in every direction, and the sun was shining."
2. " 'I dunno . . . pretty far.' "
3. "For this each man must look into his soul."

Last Lines (*poetry*)

1. Till someone find us really out.
2. But joy is wisdom, time an endless song.

HANKY-PANKY

1. Silly lily
2. Chinese knees
3. Russian mushin'
4. Mussel rustle
5. Stupid Cupid
6. Calm farm
7. Rotten cotton
8. Hipper clipper
9. Copper topper or top cop
10. Handy Andy

WHAT WOULD YOU BE DOING?

The group picked #4 as the winner. My answer was #2.

MIXED-UP MELODIES

1. G
2. J
3. F
4. A
5. I
6. B
7. D
8. E
9. C
10. H

COMPETITIVE CROSSWORDS

FILL-INS

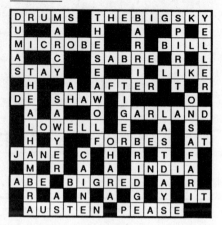

SCAVENGER HUNT

Red team #1—Beach (under the seaweed)
Blue team #1—Look under the porch
Red team #2—Climb up oak tree in back of house
Blue team #2—Cellar

WORDS WITHIN A WORD

ably	burl	cloy	lory
alar	burly	club	oary
alary	bury	coal	oral
alba	caba	cobra	orby
alco	cabal	cola	orca
arca	cala	coral	oval
arco	calory*	coryl	ovary
aula	carboy	crab	raya
aura	carl	curb	royal
aval	carob	curl	ruby
bayou	carol	curly	urva
blur	cary	curvy	valor
boar	caul	labor	vara
bola	cavy	larva	vary
bolar	claro	lava	vocal
bravo	clary	lobar	volar
bray	clay	loca	

*second spelling for *calorie*

ANIMALS IN HIDING

Solution	Animal
1. Lie in wait	lion
2. Catastrophe	cat or ass
3. New England	gnu
4. Bering	bear
5. Go for	gopher
6. Hoarse	horse
7. Austere	steer
8. Lam	lamb
9. Ceil	seal
10. Vamoose	moose

SAID THE BIRD

1. Cardinal
2. Bunting
3. Butterball
4. Blue peter
5. Red-footed booby
6. Burgomaster
7. Yellow-breasted chat
8. Chuck-will's-widow
9. Whooping crane
10. Bobwhite
11. Wild canary
12. Canvasback
13. Honeycreeper
14. Red-throated diver
15. Killdeer
16. White-tailed kite
17. Kittiwake
18. Man-o'-war
19. Mud hen
20. Nuthatch
21. Old-squaw
22. Baltimore oriole
23. Passenger pigeon
24. Quail
25. Virginia rail
26. Redhead
27. Redwing
28. Solitary sand-
    piper
29. Shoveller
30. Black skimmer
31. Starling
32. Brown thrasher
33. Whippoorwill
34. Yellowthroat
35. Swallow

MISTER 5 × 5

CRYPTOGRAMS

1. It is fitting that first-grade teachers should be able instructors.
2. The main key to all joy is: make many others truly joyous.
3. Are the people in Boston prone to spill the beans?
4. Don't take wooden nickels. Why? Because you would probably get splinters along the way.
5. To avoid a recently painted odor, put a little vanilla in your paint can.
6. Home movies often have wholesome charms for families who wish to reminisce.
7. Devout or even casual interest in sports often provides escape from troublesome problems.
8. School principal praises topnotch teacher: she has class!
9. To ward off unpleasant fumes from cigars or cigarettes, put some vinegar in a big bowl or similar vessel.
10. During slight droughts, washing my windows today always generates rain tomorrow.
11. Stern, ill-tempered landlord reprimands idle roomers.
12. Crafty supermarket shoppers watch for swollen cans or lids: poison may lurk inside.
13. Many movie directors believe rigid censors could eventually revive "big-banned era."
14. Two powerful chow dogs found in local pound got wonderful new "leashes" on life.
15. Is television evil or not? I care, yet really cannot tell.
16. Smart culinary advice: To leave hot food out for more than two hours is not very wise, we are told.
17. Each moment you inhale, you literally cause an unpoetic "inspiration."
18. Macho detective readily solved mystery on television. So what else is new?
19. By all standards, we humans should always be humane: Otherwise why are we here on earth?
20. Guests on high-ground gazebo gazed on gorgeous sight in beautiful flower garden down below.
21. Wise cooks won't thaw beef or chicken on kitchen counters because of bacteria.

22. In baseball statistics, three-base clouts are much rarer than home-run blasts.
23. Daring scuba divers observe three vicious killer sharks at close range.
24. Some clams casino recipes might require bacon slabs atop rather large quahogs.
25. Kazoos, mouth instruments of very small size, do provide fun for happy little tykes.
26. Quality may almost always be equated with worth in dollars, but not quantity.
27. Four quiet hours angling for bonefish quell seas of big troubles.
28. Uncareful urban jaywalkers, combined with unforeseen traffic jams, have often vexed many taxi drivers.
29. Those who room and eat in Hollywood homes may easily be termed "star boarders."
30. Boring lecture at our club causes great "earitation."
31. Bored lie-abed arose at noon and then had a little siesta.
32. Cars and bars brought about nought but stars and scars.
33. Oppressed teacher claimed: "The only way to shut them up is to shout them down!"
34. Do full moons affect moods of fitful canines?
35. Souped-up hotrod stirred up hipsters.
36. Which curly-haired wrestler at Grand Canyon yelled: "Gorgeous George"?
37. At best, aggression brings oppression and depression.
38. Hubby being mulish, she may logically become naggy.
39. Frosty graybeards agreed: Need often breeds degree of greed.
40. Gruff French actor detests rush in dressing for dinner scene.
41. Beer baron wanted to bring three rings to his wedding
42. Footloose older men often seem looser on the other end.
43. London paradox: Burly cops casually don bobby sox.
44. When underpinnings look like splinters, would-be sprinters should be good.
45. Chic chick nabbed in bad check rap chirped: "Cheap!"
46. Tourist seeking soft drink asked guide for "foreign ade."
47. Zoot suit on cool customer amazes trim salesman.
48. Beatnik brat took inkblot tests and labeled spots as "Pop's art."
49. Many tan he-men in T-shirts stir my Mrs.
50. Punning young punk gaily told adult: "I kid: you not."

CRYPTOCROSSWORDS

T	U	L	S	A		M	O	D	E	S
I	M	U	S	T		A	R	I	A	N
N	I	G	E	L		I	C	A	M	E
T	A	E		I	S	T		N	O	V
O	K	R	A		H	A	V	A	N	A
		C	H	A	I	M				
C	A	R	T	O	N		I	C	A	N
A	D	E		W	E	S		A	L	A
B	O	G	I	E		L	I	K	E	N
I	W	I	L	L		A	R	E	C	A
N	A	S	A	L		B	A	S	K	S

CRYPTOMATHS

Cather. Math formula: 1–2, 4–5, 7–8

Ivanhoe. Math formula: 1–4–7–10–7–4–1

SCANAGRAMS

1. canoe, ocean
2. blase, sable
3. March, charm
4. tough, ought
5. worse, swore
6. allure, laurel
7. aspire, praise
8. listen, tinsel
9. teacher, cheater
10. erupted, reputed

LITERARY SCANAGRAMS

1. remain, marine
2. Zelda, lazed
3. state, taste
4. large, Alger
5. gleans, Angel's
6. canoed, deacon
7. ropes, prose
8. goes, egos
9. pairs, Paris
10. charm, March
11. real, Lear
12. scares, caress
13. nicest, incest
14. Sartre, rarest
15. least, tales
16. beast, bates
17. scare, Acres
18. marble, Ambler
19. Siam, Amis
20. rested, desert

Answer to *That Wharton Man:*

'neath Ethan (Frome)

LIT-O-GRAMS

1. When our relatives are at home, we have to think of all their good points or it would be impossible to endure them. But when they are away, we console ourselves for their absence by dwelling on their vices.
   —Bernard Shaw, *Heartbreak House*

2. Mortals, that would follow me,
   Love Virtue, she alone is free,
   She can teach ye how to climb
   Higher than the sphery chime;
   Or, if Virtue feeble were,
   Heav'n itself would stoop to her.
   —Milton, *Comus*

3. Peace; come away; the song of woe
   Is after all an earthly song;
   Peace; come away; we do him wrong
   To sing so wildly. . .
   —Tennyson, *In Memoriam*

UNSCRAMBLE-LIT

Robert Frost
Polonius (in *Hamlet*)
Thackeray

FIRST-LETTER SCRAMBLE

Oliver Gant (in Thomas Wolfe's *Look Homeward, Angel*)
Charles Lamb
Elsinore (palace in *Hamlet*)

VERTICAL-LIT

Eugene O'Neill (third line)

LITERAQUEST

Philostrate

1. Ariel	6. Lear	11. Portia
2. Eros	7. Ophelia	12. Salerio
3. Hal	8. Peto	13. Strato
4. Hero	9. Pistol	14. Tailor
5. Iras	10. Poet	

BRIEF QUIZZES

1. Strength
2. Abstemious and facetious
3. Angry, hungry and aggry
   Aggry is an adjective designating a kind of variegated glass beads of ancient manufacture found in the Gold Coast.
   Puggry is another candidate, but its first spelling is *puggree*. It's a light scarf worn around a helmet or hat in India to protect the head from the sun.
   Both *aggry* and *puggry* are listed in *Webster's New International Dictionary,* 2d ed.
4. Woman: without her, man would be a beast.
5. Side, set and lay
   Football fans are familiar with the onside kick.

TOM SWIFTIES

1. grimly (pun on the Grimm brothers)
2. piously (pun on Pope Pius)
3. ideally (pun on ideal)
4. wisely (pun on Y's)
5. finally (wordplay: codas are finales)
6. internally (reference to interns)
7. naughtily (pun on naught—zero)
8. winsomely (wordplay: win some)
9. politely (pun on Roper's polls)
10. amply (wordplay: note that elec. and amp. are shortened forms)

MORE TOM SWIFTIES

1. chastely (pun on chased)
2. readily (pun on red)
3. charmingly (wordplay: amulets are charms)
4. starkly (naked is often preceded by stark)
5. leeringly (pun: reference to King Lear)
6. lovingly (reference to loving cups)
7. cannily (reference to cans in supermarkets)
8. rightly (pun on write)
9. sorely (pun on soar)
10. carelessly (reference to CARE packages)

HI!

SCHISM	8	AWHILE	9
SPHINX	10	ETHICS	7
OXHIDE	9	APHIDS	8
BEHIND	8	TCHICK	12
ACHING	10	UPHILL	9
		TOTAL	90

FI!

WOLFING	13	JAWFISH	12
BOWFINS	12	LOAFING	11
CONFIRM	12	WOOFING	13
COWFISH	11	CHAFING	11
COMFITS	11	PERFIDY	12
		TOTAL	118

My source for the above words is *Webster's New International Dictionary*, 2d ed. If *tchick* is new to you, it's a sound made when urging on a horse.

TRANSFERS

1. LIARS
2. OUGHT
3. TO
4. HAVE
5. GOOD
6. MEMORIES

The quotation is from *Discourses on Government*, by Algernon Sidney: 1698.

Alternate sentence based on the quotation: SOME MOVIEGOERS LAUGH. DRAT! I HOOT!

1. ET
2. TU
3. BRUTE
4. THEN
5. FALL
6. CAESAR

The quotation is from act 3, scene 1 of Shakespeare's *The Tragedy of Julius Caesar*.

THE HIDDEN WORD

1. O'Hara
2. Rent
3. Trust
4. Hash
5. Owens
6. Ebbing
7. Pebble
8. Impertinent
9. Slave
10. Tansy
11. Samuel

Hidden word: ORTHOEPISTS

1. Kitchen
2. Lamp
3. Aria
4. Bore
5. Egotist
6. Rose
7. Jail
8. Actor
9. Spades
10. Seat

Hidden word: KLABERJASS

By the way, that word is an excellent one for Fictionary. See the very first game in this book. My source for both words is the *Random House Dictionary*.

CRAZY CLUES

Three-Letter Words

1. EVE (pun)
2. ELS (there are six *L*'s in the title)
3. ELL (reference to architect Frank Lloyd Wright)
4. RAM (pun)
5. TUB (pun)
6. HAM (ham operators often work in "shacks")
7. FOX (reference to Indians)
8. ICE (pun)
9. ACT (reference to stage phrase)
10. BAA or MAA (pun on *ewe*)

Four-Letter Words

1. CENT (see any recent penny)
2. HUEY (pun on Long)
3. PLUM (reference to political plums)
4. MAYS (pun on Spring month)
5. OVEN (reference to Julia Child)
6. OVEN (pun on dough)
7. ASHE (pun)
8. BIRD (reference to Larry Bird of basketball)
9. ENDS (reference to football's tight ends)
10. NOON (wordplay)
11. HOBO (pun on Rhodes)
12. LIFE (wordplay)
13. SEED (wordplay)
14. TALL (wordplay)
15. TAME (wordplay)

Five-Letter Words

1. TOPER (wordplay)
2. LAVER (reference to tennis player Rod Laver)
3. STENO (wordplay)
4. PANTS (pun)
5. CHESS (wordplay)
6. GROOM (wordplay)
7. SCREW (wordplay)
8. ALARM (wordplay)
9. ATLAS (wordplay)
10. BAKER (pun on stollen)

Six-Letter Words

1. NETMAN (wordplay—racket)
2. CAESAR (reference to famous chef)
3. IRONER (wordplay)
4. BATTER (reference to batter's box)
5. HELMET (pun)
6. ARTIST (reference to Markham poem)
7. TELLER (wordplay)
8. TAILOR (wordplay—vested)
9. SUTTON (reference to bank robber Willie Sutton)
10. BOUNDS (wordplay)

Seven-Letter Words

1. NIAGARA (wordplay)
2. HONESTY (reference to "Honesty is the best policy")
3. TEACHER (wordplay—class)
4. BOARDER (reference to star boarder)
5. TRANSIT (pun: *"sic transit gloria mundi"*)

MATCH GAME

1. f	6. e	
2. d	7. i	
3. h	8. a	
4. j	9. c	
5. b	10. g	

TITLE SEARCHES

1. *A Farewell to Arms*
2. *Total Fitness*
3. "La Vie en Rose"

RHYMING CLUES

1. VIEW	6. ROLE	
2. ERR	7. ORAL	
3. OVER	8. NEST	
4. TIRE	9. ASPIRIN	
5. HIRED	10. RIGHT	

TANGLED JINGLES: CLUES

1. To enumerate is to *count*.
   The second line refers to Rhode Island Reds, or *chickens*.
2. "Sweet desires" are *wishes*.
   "Mendicants" are *beggars*.
3. "Pegasus" is a *horse*.
   "Enamel" refers to *teeth*.
4. "Moonlight" refers to *night*.
   The "lovely creature of the court" is a *lady*.
5. The first line refers to *children*.
   Puns on *scene* (seen) and *herd* (heard).
6. The "boxers" are *dogs*.
   "Lying flat" is a hint that they are *sleeping*.
7. The first line refers to a *purse* or *wallet*.
   The "greens" are *dollars*. The last line refers to Andrew Jackson, who won a great battle at New Orleans in the War of 1812.
8. The "cage of clay" is a *court for a sport*.
   The last line contains wordplay on *love*.
9. "Xyloid" means *wooden*.
   "Score" equals *twenty*. "One" refers to *dollar*.
10. The first line is poesy for *life*.
    "Pottery" alludes to a *bowl* in this context.
11. "Dominion" equals *reign*. Pun: *reign-rain*
    "Oxford sheen" equals *shine*. Oxfords are shoes.
12. "Remorse" suggests *repent*.
    "Mercury" suggests speed or *haste*.
13. "Lactic" means *milky*. The "donor" is a *cow*.
    "Bay" is a bay horse, which is *brown*.
    "More than soon" means *now*.
14. *How* is a friendly greeting once given to and by Indians.
    The second line means, *Are you fixed?*

TANGLED JINGLES

1. Don't count your chickens before they're hatched.
2. If wishes were horses, beggars would ride.
3. Don't look a gift horse in the mouth.
4. Who was that lady I saw you with last night? That was no lady—that was my wife.
5. Children should be seen and not heard.
6. Let sleeping dogs lie.
7. Have you got change of a twenty?
8. Anyone for tennis?
9. Don't take any wooden nickels.
10. Life is just a bowl of cherries.
11. Come rain or come shine.
12. Marry in haste; repent at leisure.
13. How now, brown cow?
14. How are you fixed for blades? (old Gillette commercial)

CONVERSIONS

1. ARM-AIM-AID-LID-LED-LEG
2. RIVER-RAVER-WAVER-WATER
3. GIVE-GAVE-LAVE-LAKE-TAKE
4. RAKE-TAKE-TALE-TALL-TOLL-TOOL
5. FISH-FIST-FAST-CAST-COST-COAT-BOAT
6. BEAR-BOAR-BOOR-BOON-LOON-LION
7. STAR-SOAR-SOUR-POUR-POOR-POON*-MOON
8. HARP-HARE-HIRE-LIRE-LYRE
9. TREE-TREY-GREY-GREW-GROW-CROW-CROP-CHOP
10. BEAT-BLAT-FLAT-FLAG-FLOG

OFF WITH ITS HEAD!

1. STALE-TALE-ALE
2. CRATE-RATE-ATE
3. BLADE-LADE-ADE
4. CHAIR-HAIR-AIR
5. TIRED-IRED-RED
6. BLINK-LINK-INK
7. SPEAR-PEAR-EAR
8. FRAIL-RAIL-AIL
9. SHELL-HELL-ELL
10. SMALL-MALL-ALL

Challenger Answer: PRELATE

WHAT, NO VOWELS!

nth (as in to the nth degree)

PDQ means "pretty damned quick." It's a relative of ASAP ("as soon as possible").

LIMERICKS

And as for the bucket, Nantucket.
1. But whenever I see her, I laffe.
2. But not so you'd notice it much.
3. The dik-dik continued to tik-tik.
4. I really can't say. I forget.

P-T FLEET

PAINTY	PETITE	POLITY
PALATE	PEYOTE	POTATO
PARITY	PINITE	PRESTO
PEDATA	PIRATE	PRETTY
PEDATE	PLENTY	PRONTO
PELITE	PLINTH	PUPATE
PELOTA	POINTY	PURITY
PESETA	POLITE	PYRITE

BRAIN GAMES

I.

1. POLE (antelope)
2. DIRT (strident)
3. EWER (farewell)
4. VEIL (believer)
5. TING (dignitary)
6. MINI (liniment)
7. TUBE (debutante)
8. MAIL (parliament)

II.

1. pearl
2. amethyst
3. beryl
4. topaz
5. diamond
6. opal

III.

1. Some kids are hard to put up with.
2. Content yourself with one pancake this morning.
3. Most students drew a blank on question two.
4. My hand's number than my five fingers.

*E. Indian tree

5. These lovely paintings you have entrance me.
6. The medium heard voices from the
   beyond.

IV.
1. snap, crackle and pop
2. hook, line and sinker
3. man, woman and child
4. red, white and blue
5. sun, moon and stars
6. stop, look and listen
7. ready, willing and able
8. game, set and match
9. hop, skip and jump
10. beg, borrow and steal
11. wine, women and song

PALINDROME

STAR COMEDY BY DEMOCRATS

BRIEF INTERLUDE

1. Bookkeeper
2. I'm O.K., are you?
3. Water, or H_2O (H to O)
4. Herein (he, her, here, ere, re, rein, in)

REBUSES

1. Ten below zero
2. Diamond in the rough
3. Do you understand?
4. Man(n) overboard
5. Pi (pie) in the sky
6. See through the plot
7. Man(n) about town
8. One in a mil-lion
9. Runabout car
10. Horses around

RIDDLES

1. He shrinks from washing
2. A little before Eve
3. Because they mew till late (mutilate)

4. When he plans a head
5. B natural
6. Ashes
7. The shortest day
8. Ohio
9. The sun
10. When they are pared (paired)
11. It goes from mouth to mouth
12. One baits his hooks; the other hates his books
13. They make people good for nothing
14. Expediency (X P D N C)
15. Chessmen
16. Your picture
17. His nose
18. Because the queen is not a subject
19. It may make them mean—me(a)n
20. The sooner it is put out, the better

1. It takes the frog forty-three days. He gains 1
   foot each day until the forty-second day; on
   that night he is 3 feet from the top. The next
   morning he leaps out and does not fall back.
2. The man takes the goose over first. He returns
   and takes the fox and brings the goose back
   with him. He leaves it and crosses the river
   with the corn. Finally he returns with the goose
   Question: Why doesn't the fox run away?
   One has to assume he's been tamed!
3. The visitor was the prisoner's son.

VOUGHT RIDDLES

1. Cuckoopint
2. Band-Aid
3. A pound
4. Belly button
5. Good growing conditions

THE LICENSE GAME

1. Exiguous
2. Azimuth
3. Panjandrum
4. Obloquy
5. Chophouse
6. Polemic
7. Kumquat
8. Mythomania
9. Pibroch
10. Hyaline or phylum

My answer to #5 reminds me of an old verbal
trick. Ask a friend to pronounce *cho-pho-use*. He
will be tempted to say *cho'fo-use*.

OLD GLORY

A. Red tape
B. White water

A. "Blue Skies"
B. Red herring

A. White sale
B. "Blue Boy"

A. "Roses are red. . ."
* B. Paul Whiteman

A. Monte Blue
B. Red as a beet

A. White as a sheet
B. Out of the blue

A. "Red Sails in the Sunset"
B. Theodore White

A. "Am I Blue?"
B. Red Skelton

A. Great White Way
B. Blue Monday

A. Red Buttons
B. Whitewall tires

A. Bluebird
B. "The Lady in Red"

A. "Whizzer" White
B. Bluebells

A. In the red
B. Whitey Ford

A. "Blues in the Night"
B. Red Sea

A. White Sea
B. Bluebonnet

A. Red Schoendeinst
B. Whitewash

A. Like a blue streak
B. Little Red Riding Hood

A. Black and white
B. Bluefin

A. Red Ryder (of comics)
B. Tennis whites

A. Ben Blue
B. Red Barber

A. Whitecaps
B. "Blue Suede Shoes"

A. Washington Redskins
B. Whitelaw Reid

A. "Little Boy Blue"
B. Redwood tree

A. "The whites of their eyes"
B. "Ole Blue Eyes"

A. Red Jacket
B. As white as snow

A. Blue dart
B. Redcoats

A. White Plains, N.Y.
B. Blueprint

A. Red Square
B. Wave the white flag

A. Blue laws
B. The Red Baron

A. Pearl White
B. Blue jeans

AT THIS POINT A GAVE UP!

THE A-A GAME

1. RADAR
2. MADAM
3. ALARM
4. PANDA
5. LIANA

SENSIBLE SENTENCES

1. Did you soak your sock in soap and water to make this mock turtle soup?
2. I'll bet that mink coat cost a mint! Are you headed for the Arctic? All we get here is a light mist at most.
3. Larry Parks played many parts, but would have been miscast as Marty—the loner at every party, who wanted to marry.
4. Come July, I expect to be duly summoned for jury duty.
5. It was not a dead heat. Galloping Shoes won by a head.

ACROSTIC

(W.) SOMERSET MAUGHAM:
CAKES AND ALE

Hypocrisy is the most difficult and nerve-racking vice that any man can pursue; it needs an unceasing vigilance and a rare detachment of spirit. It cannot, like adultery or gluttony, be practiced in spare moments; it is a whole-time job.

A	Spirit	N	Aesop
B	Overbearing	O	McCarthy
C	Minuit	P	Contiguity
D	Eccentricity	Q	Affront
E	Randomly	R	Kittiwake
F	Slabs	S	Earthshine
G	Elective	T	Senses
H	Toucan	U	Adjutant
I	Midge	V	Ninny
J	Appointed	W	Dice
K	Unnatural	X	Andromache
L	Grief	Y	Laves
M	Hind	Z	Ectoplasm

THE FIRST CROSSWORD PUZZLE

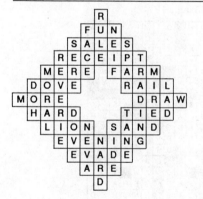

MALESKA'S FIRST PUBLISHED PUZZLE

CLOTHES LINE

1924 CONTEST PUZZLE

PUZZLE CUM PUNS

```
SABOT  MAFIA  DRABS
CZECHMATING  BERET
RUSSIANBEAR  AFIRE
ORT SHEA  NAE  ILLE
DESI  DAY  FLENSED
    BAIT  BAFFIN
SCANT  EDILE  RIATA
UHR  LEREVE  JESTER
LAIT  ASTARTE  HONE
UNSHOD  ALCOTT  NON
STEAM  GIVEN  INERT
    INHALE  OSLO
CASSIUS  BAA   DISC
APOC  MPS  OVUM  DEA
SALON  INDIANOCEAN
URARE  PERSIANLAMB
STREW  EDSEL  SISSY
```

PENNIES FOR YOUR THOUGHTS

```
¢IPEDE  VIN¢  TSP  PAEAN
ARARAT  INNO¢III   UNCLE
UMLAUT  CAESAREA  RE¢LY
RAMS  UPIN   VEG   LEAR
  ELBA  ENROSE  UNRIPE
SCARERS  IOS   AME   CAL
CASSIUS  RPI  PARIS  INA
EVA  STUKAS  GRAINS  TET
NEIL  EPIC  COARSE  PYLE
ERNES  EKEOUT   ESAU
INTHEFIVEANDTEN¢STORE
ALAS  TRIALS   HIRED
S¢ER  MOMENT  ETNA  TIPI
TUX  MILERS  DREARY  GAT
OPP  ALDAS  LES  STOMACH
ILA  GIE   RAF   SHRINKS
CETANE  ADESTE   OREL
IRIS  ROT   MINI   LAMP
SCARF  AMNIOTIC  TAILOR
ALTAI  CON¢RATE  IN¢IVE
CRES¢  ¢RE  BUSS  SYSTEM
```

DIAGRAMLESS PUZZLE

```
  ARAB
SNORE  PEN
ENACT  AGO  CUB
REST  ROUTINE
EXTINCT  NADIR
  COLIN  METE
TAG  TACIT  RET
OGRE  PILOT
TIARA  PENALTY
ALFALFA  MARE
LET  TAT  APRIL
  ODE  REGAL
    TROD
```

CONCISE ADVICE

Think much, speak little and write less.
—Italian proverb

```
AYER  ATTU   STEP
COME  IRAS   ARNO
THINKMUCHSPEAK
SOREN  NOEL   ETE
    WORK  RUINED
GPS   LOCKERS
LITTLEAND   LEUC
ILIE  LEO   ANNA
SOLAR  LEUD  GIR
STERES   TOLIVE
APT  CHAP  MONEL
DITA  OAR  LERE
ENOS  WRITELESS
   PREENER  RES
BURSAR   CAAN
ANE  MCII  TEMPO
ITALIANPROVERB
RIDE  PTAH  EROO
DEED  SOLO  REAL
```

STEPQUOTE

Matrimony is not a word; it's a sentence.
—Eddie Cantor, as quoted in *Reader's
Digest,* March, 1934.

```
MATRIM  DAMP  COW
OVERDO  ODOR  ALA
REASON  DEMEANED
ERR  NYLON  CUTIE
  ARTIE  HERONS
CARO  SNO  ADORE
AGOOD  STALER
ROUTES  ANT  ASTA
ERN  SPAWNED  PER
WADS  ADO  REPINE
  CARERS  BENET
DARTS  DIT  ESTE
PIRATE  OSAKA
AGAPE  CONAN  YOM
CEMENTED  SERAPE
ASI  DOTE  ENURED
STS  SEER  NTENCE
```

SLIDE-QUOTE

There is no good but God.
—Koran

```
TABS   GAVEL    HOMERS
OHOH LATERAL  OMELET
ASEA ASTRIDE  RENATA
TORRES  IVE  SINN   TIT
   DESIRE FINE  CIRE
WES  LINE  SOON  SHOER
ENTREES  INON  STANDS
ADEER  ENROL   DEEP
SURF   ROOD  VITA   ARI
ERETZ  TINGLES  KORAN
LEO  OVER   ROTO   BAWL
   COED  MANOR  DOBIE
SOVIET  WISE  DUELIST
UNITY  MASS   WEBB   AHS
GARY  FIST   POROUS
ADA  BUSH  SAM  ATTICS
RIGORS   ELEMENT  AGHA
EMOTES   DIVINES  GOON
DESTRY   VERSE    STUD
```

CIRCLES IN THE SQUARE

I think I think, therefore I think I am.
—Ambrose Bierce, from "The
  Devil's Dictionary"

```
LUCIT  HIDES   SPANK
ERICA  ORALE   EAMON
NOTED  MACKE   DRONE
ANIS   LITHE  BIERCE
PIE   INEE  KIT   EEL
ECSTASY    AERIE
    HIT  DICTIONARY
ADHERE   ALEC   NISEI
VEER  DALETHS   STEP
ELLES  ALTA   AFLAME
CAMINOREAL     VIE
   NONOS   CANDIDA
THE  WEN   PLAN   SER
RECESS   SAINT   ROVE
ALLAH  KARAT   ROBIN
LEAVE  INONE   ITALO
ANTED  MOLAR   FIRST
```

U-QUOTE

No, you never get any fun
Out of the things you haven't done.
—Ogden Nash, from "Portrait of the Artist as a
  Prematurely Old Man"

BOXQUOTE

That must be very fine; I don't understand it in the least!
—Molière, from "Le Médecin Malgré Lui" II.iv.

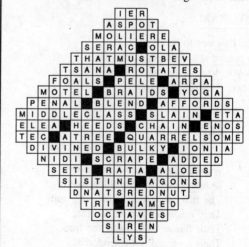

STORY CROSSWORD   CRYPTOCROSSWORD

CRYPTIC CROSSWORD

PUNS AND ANAGRAMS

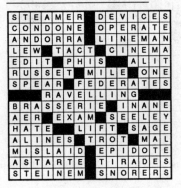

ACROSS

1 Double meaning
4 Red (Moscow) + actor (performs on stage)
10 Double meaning
11 Cat (awkward act*) + a + log (record)
12 Pun
13 Cent (penny); rely (trust); re-cent-ly
15 Fir (evergreen) + st (little street)
18 Indus(try) = trade
19 Has a nice *
22 Double meaning, pun
24 Double meaning
25 A pistol (homophone)
26 Re (in the matter of) + le (the French) + gate
    (door)
27 Double meaning

DOWN

1 C (hundred) + lobbers (tennis players)
2 Of sOME GAmes
3 Chicken (cowardly) + dumpling (stocky
    person)
5 S(outhern) peace *
6 Pun on mint
7 Levis (blue jeans) + Tees (river): te-levis-es
8 Regal (splendid) + e
9 Rep(resentative) + tile (flooring material)
14 Con (criminal) + genial (pleasant)
16 Double meaning
17 Double meaning
20 Est (is in Latin) + her (girl)
21 Homophone: black Knight/night
23 City ReNATA Lives in

ESPYGRAM

When I aspired to be a father,
You praised my willingness to bother.
Now you despair; you never knew
I'd leave the diapers to you.

ESPYRAMID

A worm once in an apple grew;
An old man bit the worm in two
(A mean and naughty thing to do).
The two halves named him in a suit.
They made demand he restitute
Their former state inside the fruit.
Their lot could not amended be,
Which maddened them, as it would me.